graze

graze

Inspiration for Small Plates
and Meandering Meals

SUZANNE
LENZER

Photography by
Nicole Franzen

RODALE.

RODALE wellness

Live happy. Be healthy. Get inspired.

Sign up today to get exclusive access to our authors, exclusive bonuses,
and the most authoritative, useful, and cutting-edge information on health,
wellness, fitness, and living your life to the fullest.

Visit us online at RodaleWellness.com
Join us at RodaleWellness.com/Join

Rodale books may be purchased for business or promotional use or for special sales.
For information, please write to:
Trade Books/Special Markets Department, Rodale, Inc., 733 Third Avenue, New York, NY 10017

Printed in China

Rodale Inc. makes every effort to use acid-free ∞, recycled paper ♻.

Book design by Rae Ann Spitzenberger
Photography by Nicole Franzen
Prop stylist: Kate Jordan
Food stylist: Suzanne Lenzer
Food stylist assistants: Erica Clark and Kate Schmidt

Library of Congress Cataloging-in-Publication Data is on file with publisher.

ISBN-13: 978–1–62336–753–4 hardcover

Distributed to the trade by Macmillan

2   4   6   8   10   9   7   5   3   1   hardcover

RODALE

Follow us @RodaleBooks on

We inspire health, healing, happiness, and love in the world.
Starting with you.

"There is a kind of appealing grace in having
the end result of a project, food or otherwise,
seemingly brought off without strain."

—LEE BAILEY

An Inspired Platter of Fruit and a Piece of Chocolate (PAGE 154)

contents

introduction

I WOULD LOVE TO BE *THAT* GIRL. THE ONE WHO RIDES A MOTORCYCLE, GOES OUT with a painter or a rock star, or better, a restless surfer; the one shooting pool, singing karaoke, dancing on the bar; the one whose life is one beautiful adventure after another, never the same thing twice. She travels the world (probably has a bikini and a ball gown in her designer bag at all times); she's seen the Sahara and been to the Bhutan. She speaks five—maybe six—languages, has a degree in philosophy, and might even be a spy. Oh, and she has amazing hair.

But I'm not her. While she's out living dangerously, I'm standing by the stove stirring risotto, or peeling a hard-boiled egg over the sink for lunch. When she's sitting down to a dinner of oysters and Champagne, I'm crawling into bed with a cup of a tea and a big orange cat. It's just the way things turned out and I'm okay with it. Without all the glamorous distractions, I learned how to cook.

My consolation for not being a rock star, Nobel Prize winner, world-renowned neurosurgeon, or the next Bond girl is that I get to play with fire and knives in the comfort of my own kitchen. As a food stylist and passionate cook, I get to have my own dazzling adventures: the soufflé that rose perfectly, the sauce that curdled horribly. I too can experience the vastness of the world simply by what I cook and eat. No, I may not be a free spirit in the world at large, but I've been fortunate to visit at least a handful of far-off lands, sample some regional delicacies, and learn a bit about culinary tradition. Now my inner adventuress comes out in my kitchen, where I choose to taste a bit here and a bit there, feast on flavors from all over the world, and wander happily from one bite to the next. I am, admittedly, a culinary wanderer, a vagabond, a gypsy, a self-proclaimed grazer. Someone who cooks all day for a living and then can't wait (most of the time) to cook something wonderful on the weekends too. When I cook for myself and for friends, I want the preparation to be easy but the presentation to be lovely. I want the dishes I make to be multiple so there's something for everyone, and I want them all to work together; a meal like this should have a sensibility, a theme, an aesthetic, like an eclectically decorated room that you don't want to leave.

When I go out to eat, I'm happiest with a menu that lets me pick from a little of this and a little of that, to share a selection of smaller dishes, whether it's just two of us or a crowd. And while cooking at home is rarely as extravagant (often a homemade pizza and a salad is our dinner of choice), when I do cook more elaborate meals, I want to offer something other than the expected meat with a vegetable or starch. I want to enjoy a similar, albeit simplified, menu to those I enjoy in my favorite restaurants. Whether the dishes I pull together are simply well-chosen ingredients left nearly naked (think a good Spanish sardine from a tin laid seductively over a cracker with a squeeze of lemon) or something that requires a bit more energy on the part of the cook (a quick melon soup with toasted prosciutto shards), I love a couple of well-curated dishes that make the meal more of a celebration than just sustenance.

When my husband, Ken, and I first went to Spain, we fell deeply, wholeheartedly in love with tapas, so much so that we ate nothing else—not a single full meal—the entire trip. So giddy over the breadth of individual bites at our disposal, so enchanted were we by this natural rhythm of consumption, that when we got home, our entire style of eating changed. We were both happier and more comfortable nibbling on a plate of cheese, sharing a dish of olive oil–fried shrimp, and chatting over a slice of grilled bread than eating a huge bowl of pasta or a steak. No, we don't eat this way every night. As I've said, many nights we make a small pizza and a salad, but even that in its own way is a form of grazing for us. We snack on a piece of Parma ham as we wash the lettuce, savor a bit of Taleggio before it makes its way onto the crust, and Ken is famous (at least in our house) for devouring all the crispy croutons and delicate petals of Parmesan in the Caesar salad before it's even dressed.

Grazing is not a new idea—in Greece, it's the notion behind the mezze; and, as I've said, Spain has tapas; Japanese sushi is not dissimilar; and the Italian *cicchetti* is all about small, varied dishes. To me, the concept is irresistible: *consuming less of more*. What could be more stimulating for a cook or an eater? And yes, while there are those who might say grazing is akin to snacking and, in turn, an unhealthy way to eat constantly instead of mindfully, I beg to differ. Grazing is about consciously eating small portions of multiple dishes made with thought and intent.

I find the notion of grazing to be liberating; it frees us as cooks from the pressure of a main course, alleviates the expectations of what comes first, second, and what goes on the side. Just imagine: a plate of figs, some spiced baby lamb chops, and a few pieces of roasted Delicata squash on a crisp fall day; a shooter of spiced tomato bisque alongside a toasted Brie crostini and a smattering of cured meat as a late-winter lunch; a platter of grilled sardines served with slabs of toasted bread, blistered cherry tomatoes, and pickled fennel, followed by a spoonful of milky panna cotta on a blazing hot day by the sea; a slice of buttery toast and a cup of potato-leek soup supped while standing at the counter with a friend. Each of these is a medley of little dishes pulled together to create something collectively more delicious. Something that embraces the notion of the seasons, that's inspired by what's ripe and most flavorful at that particular moment. And while it may sound effortful, the truth is, grazing is as much about the shopping as the cooking; if you plan well, you'll find that you actually spend less time in front of the stove.

keeping it simple

Putting out a few small dishes seems harder than just one, I know. But the key is to embrace good ingredients that need minimal help from the cook and to dispose of the idea that you have to make everything yourself—smart shopping, a bit of planning, and confidence is really all it takes. It also helps to think of what you feel like eating rather than spend hours digging around for the perfect recipe. When I cook at home, instead of seeking out a recipe and following it, I do almost exactly the opposite. I think about what I'm in the mood for or have on hand and work backward from there. Rarely do I follow an entire recipe verbatim—I cherry-pick a little from a curated collection, choosing the mix of ingredients that sounds good to me and the blend of techniques that makes the most sense.

I steer clear of recipes that call for multiple bowls and pans in favor of simpler, more streamlined approaches—or I figure out how to simplify them myself (a small kitchen is a great motivator for keeping dinner contained). Erica, a close friend who also cooks professionally, swears that if she's reading a recipe and a candy thermometer is required, she immediately turns the page. All cooks have a limit, a mental barrier that renders a recipe too complex or too laden to bother with; hers is the requisite candy thermometer while mine is subject to my mood, but too many pots, pans, and gadgets is certainly up there on my list. I also won't buy esoteric ingredients that are needed for only a teaspoon or a drizzle; even if your pantry isn't perfectly stocked, there's almost always a way to substitute a few ground fennel seeds for fennel pollen or a mix of brown sugar and lime juice for tamarind paste when you need to.

I can also be driven to distraction by recipes that call for "a tablespoon of garlic," "1 cup basil," or "¾ pound tomatoes." Bothering to figure out how many cloves of garlic make up a tablespoon (two small or one large, but what if all I have seems to be medium?) drives me mad. And what exactly does a cup of basil look like? Are the leaves packed or just lightly squished in there? And perhaps more importantly, how does the recipe writer know if I like more or less garlic or basil? This is why many of the recipes you'll find here—when the amounts really don't impact the outcome of the dish, just the intensity of a certain flavor—call for "a handful" of this or "3 to 4 sprigs" of that. When it comes to fresh vegetables, you'll also see "1 large or 2 medium tomatoes, chopped (about 2 cups)" instead of "¾ pound tomatoes, chopped." Even after years of cooking, I still haven't the foggiest idea what ¾ pound of tomatoes is; in midsummer, it could probably be one large, but in deepest winter, perhaps three small. As for the garlic and herbs, I trust you, the cook and the eater, to have some sense of how you want your food to taste. And you should trust you, too. As home cooks, we aren't trying to replicate the same meal for 20 tables every night—we're just trying to make good food that we want to eat, and have some fun along the way.

pairing food, or what goes with what

One reason I believe many of us are more comfortable with the idea of small plates when we eat at a restaurant is how seamlessly they fit together; the menu, if it's done well, will maintain a singular sensibility, a cohesive aesthetic—a selection of dishes that all complement one another in terms of flavor and texture. At a restaurant, the chef has done the thinking for us, making it easy to choose what to eat without consciously thinking about "what goes with what."

Of course, when we cook at home, we have to think about how dishes work together, but a roast chicken and garlic mashed potatoes or a bowl of pasta is considerably easier to navigate than a table of six dishes. Part of the art of creating food for grazing comes with understanding which foods play well together. Certainly you can mix and mingle anything you like, and you should (your taste and mine may not be the same and what we have in the fridge and pantry most certainly varies too), but there is a logic and beauty to pairing food in a way that makes sense.

The way I decide what to serve with what is like a puzzle. I start with an idea for one dish, usually the most time- and labor-intensive of the meal, and then I try to

FACING PAGE: *Spanish Tortilla with Sweet Onion and Thyme* (PAGE 120) | *Fresh Figs with Serrano Ham* (PAGE 10) | *Blistered Shishito Peppers with Flaky Salt* (PAGE 73) | *Pan con Tomate* (PAGE 43)

figure out what subsequent and simple dishes fit around that first one. Most of those secondary dishes are chosen because they either require minimal cooking or are simply good-quality store-bought provisions. Sometimes in the midst of figuring out what to make, the original key player changes to better suit the others I've become attached to, and that's okay. It's a process of moving the pieces around until a fully formed picture comes into view, and I can see how the dishes will live together on the table and how they'll taste together. And while it sounds like an involved process, this all usually takes place in less than 5 minutes while standing in the produce aisle or wandering the stands at the farmers' market.

There are a few different ways of approaching what to cook and serve with what. First, there's seasonality. If you start by thinking about what ingredients are in-season at the same time, you'll have a pretty good idea of what goes together thematically: asparagus and peas; winter squash and apples; corn, tomatoes, and grilled seafood; fresh goat cheese and plums or cherries. These pairings make sense because they're ripe and available at the same time. With this strategy in mind, you can see how, come spring, deep-fried asparagus will work beautifully with a small dish of minted pea soup and a plate of smoked salmon. Or how once fall arrives, a sweet onion and chard toast would be the ideal companion for a dish of roasted Brussels sprouts with pancetta and pecans or a cup of cassoulet. Mother Nature directs us to what we should make, or at least gives us a really smart starting point, so following the seasons makes coming up with a menu incredibly easy.

Regionality is another really simple way to craft a grazing meal. Feel like something Spanish? Start with a *tortilla*, add some *jamón*, olives, *pan con tomate*, and a dish of briny anchovies or fried chickpeas. More in the mood for Middle Eastern? Let spiced lamb chops serve as the anchoring dish surrounded by a bowl of eggplant mousse, a plate of olives, and some sun-dried tomatoes. It's not hard to pair different dishes together once you start thinking in terms of where foods originate.

Another slightly more creative way to come up with food pairings is to deconstruct more complex meals. Take a favorite of mine: pizza with prosciutto, artichokes, and olives. Why not just eliminate the crust (and the cooking) and set out these three ingredients on the table with a loaf of good bread and a dish of olive oil for dipping? I have a passion for cassoulet; if I take it apart, a meal of sliced sausage, marinated beans, oven-roasted tomatoes, and a good loaf of bread becomes a nice hint at those alluring flavors without all the fuss. When you think about classic preparations, reduce them to their essential elements, and then rearrange and simplify them, you have another clever method for creating an inspired grazing meal. And, when all else fails, turn to page xxxii to take a peek at the menus there.

how i shop

Food shopping is something I enjoy. I know this isn't true for everyone, but the way I look at it, picking out the food I'm going to make is just as important as cooking it; the same care and thought that go into chopping that garlic or peeling that squash should go into choosing it. Certainly I could whip through the grocery store, grabbing bags and boxes of prepackaged stuff, but where's the thoughtful intent in that?

The way I procure food may not be ideal or even possible for you, but it can give you a sense of what makes for an efficient and relatively waste-free kitchen. So here's my general routine: I do a weekly staples trip to the grocery store for the basics—milk for coffee, bananas and berries for granola in the morning, greens and other vegetables for salads and such, and yogurt, butter, eggs, and so on (the stuff we go through weekly).

At the same time, I'll pick up olives and marinated artichokes in the deli section, decent crackers or grissini, and whatever else we've finished off during the week and need to replenish. I'd rather buy these specialty items at our local Italian delicatessen and cheese shop, and sometimes I do, but I'd be lying if I said I made a trip every week just for these special provisions. For fresh mozzarella, prosciutto, and other charcuterie, I do try to get to our favorite Italian spot, but if I don't, the weekly shop has to do, and I don't lose sleep over it.

I do buy my fish from the fish store and most of my meat from the butcher. I'm lucky to have a great fish store (The Lobster Place) and a wonderful butcher (Ottomanelli) within walking distance of our apartment, and for me, these two trips are important. I like knowing my fishmonger and my butcher, and they guide me in terms of what's freshest, in-season, well-aged, or the best value. I like that Frank, my butcher, is happy to order something for me if I need it, butterfly a bird if I ask, and trim or tie up a roast for me while I stand by happily chatting. Could I do it myself? Sure, but it's easier to ask him; he does an infinitely better job, and I learn a ton just by standing on the other side of his counter watching him work.

Then there's the farmers' market. I can spend an hour or more wandering the Union Square market in New York City, taking in the breadth of fresh fruit and vegetables and breathing in the overt scent of dirt and produce, the aroma of which always catches me off guard in the midst of such blatantly urban surroundings. But I'm partial to the farm stand near our cottage in Connecticut. Once summer arrives, I am devoted to my Friday afternoon stop for corn and peaches and tomatoes and zucchini and leeks and whatever else they have on display. I know it sounds like so much foodie nonsense to wax poetic about the difference in produce between the grocery store and the farmers' market or farm stand, but for anyone who's tasted corn just picked that morning or bitten into a peach fresh off the tree, you know that I'm not being pretentious—there is a difference. That said, I am hardly above buying corn at the grocery store if it's just in from Georgia and the local stuff hasn't arrived yet. (I love my grocery store, and pretty much everything in this book can be found at a decent one if you don't have a farmers' market, butcher, or specialty shop at your disposal.)

But if you have access and can afford it, taking advantage of (and supporting) the local guys is worthwhile. It's also a strategy I use to keep me honest when it comes to cooking seasonally; if you're buying ingredients that are truly at their peak, fresh, and flavorful, then you don't need a lot of added flavors to enhance them. I'd be fibbing if I said I didn't buy asparagus from South America in January when I've already eaten my weight in potatoes and winter squash and need a pre-spring boost, but I try to be true to the seasonal ethic, and when I am, the food needs far less fiddling. And that's really the point of cooking for me: tasting the ingredients in their purest, freshest, most naked, radiant, and unadulterated form. A glug of olive oil and a sprinkle of salt and pepper are frequently all that's needed to turn good ingredients into a glorious meal. It's all about what you can rationalize and what makes sense for you.

the grazer's larder: stocking the pantry, fridge, and freezer

I have to come clean here and say that I dislike those utilitarian sections in cookbooks that adamantly list what tools or ingredients I should have in my kitchen. There's something doctrinaire and restrictive about them—as if by not having everything on the list, my capabilities in the kitchen are somehow limited, my expertise lessened; after a single glance, I'm always exhausted by all I lack—and how much energy it would take to remedy the situation.

No, I don't have a set of pots and pans in every size (where would I keep them?); I've never had a microwave and don't miss it (it strikes me as most useful for reheating coffee); I don't own a food mill or a ricer, a toaster or a juicer—the list goes on and on. Yet none of these things keep me from cooking, and *not* having some of them actually means I have to get more creative. If you want to make a pie and don't have a rolling pin, I can assure you from personal experience that a wine bottle works just fine. A chicken can be roasted on a baking sheet if you don't have a proper roasting pan; and while I love my mandoline, I've only recently gotten one, and for years was able to slice things quite nicely with a plain old knife. Cooking and eating reasonably well isn't contingent upon stocking your kitchen with a lot of fussy pans, utensils, gadgets you'll rarely use (if you can even find them when you need them), a bunch of rarified spices, or a pantry full of different types of flour. Rather, I think being a good cook has more to do with an instinct for flavors and a sense of bravery—being open to trying new things—than anything else.

With that little diatribe out of the way, I must confess that now you're going to get a list, but a very loosey-goosey one. The way that I like to eat is largely dependent upon keeping my pantry well-stocked with my favorite basics as well as special bits and pieces that can be pulled out to compose a meal with almost no work beyond the slice of a knife or the twist of lid. This being the grazing cook's quintessential parlor trick—a pantry of diverse and delectable provisions—I can't help but offer a list for illustration. Don't think of this list as a mandate by any means; what I like and keep on hand may not be what you like. Instead, think of it as a glimpse into my pantry and freezer (a very chaotic and often less-than-well-organized affair), an example of how to make grazing a more natural way of eating.

PANTRY

Olive oil

Sea salt (finely ground)

Maldon sea salt flakes

Sherry vinegar (or red or white wine vinegar)

Balsamic vinegar

Dijon mustard (classic and country-style)

Pasta

San Marzano tomatoes

Grissini (thin breadsticks; packaged is fine)

Crackers or flatbreads

Canned gigante beans

Canned black beans

Canned chickpeas

Canned cannellini beans

Anchovies

Sardines

Pepperoncini

Sun-dried tomatoes

Nuts (almonds, pecans, pistachios, walnuts, etc.)

Mayonnaise

Soy sauce

Thai fish sauce

Toasted sesame oil

Chili sauce or paste

All-purpose flour

Baking powder and soda

Sugar (granulated, brown [dark or light], and powdered)

Active dry yeast

FRUIT AND VEGETABLE STAPLES

Garlic

Lemons

Limes

Onions and shallots

Avocados

Tomatoes

Arugula or other tender greens

Fresh herbs* (rosemary, thyme, basil, tarragon, mint, oregano, and bay leaves)

I grow small pots of these so I always have some on hand—it's heartbreaking to buy whole bunches and let them go to waste. If you don't have the room or inclination to start a few pots, the resinous herbs like rosemary and thyme will keep longer in the fridge, while the tender herbs can be chopped and frozen in small plastic bags.

FRIDGE

Eggs

Butter (salted and unsalted)

Olives of varying kinds

Marinated artichoke hearts

Parmesan cheese

A soft cheese you like (I tend to have a round of goat's milk Brie or a hunk of Taleggio on hand)

A harder cheese you like (A good English cheddar or Stilton and a wedge of Manchego or Pyrénées Brebis are some of my regulars)

Bacon (thick-cut)

Prosciutto, soppressata, or some type of charcuterie

Smoked salmon

FREEZER

Frozen peas

Frozen fruit (stuff going soft that gets cleaned, cut, and bagged)

Frozen spinach

Breadcrumbs

Mozzarella (bought fresh and frozen in small bits)

Italian sausages

Pancetta

Leftovers of all kinds

SPICES

Black pepper in a peppermill

Red chili flakes

Pimentón (smoked paprika)

Fennel seeds

Old Bay seasoning

Ground cumin

Ground coriander

Cayenne pepper

Ground ginger

Ground turmeric

Vanilla extract

Almond extract

the essential stuff

life is better with bread
(and crackers, grissini, etc.)

I love bread. I make bread regularly and eat bread daily. I don't understand the trend of demonizing gluten. I completely understand that some people can't tolerate it, and that's incredibly sad, but for those who don't actually suffer from celiac disease or a gluten intolerance, you're missing out.

If you like to bake, there are few things more satisfying than turning out a loaf of homemade bread. Whether you take on the project of making your own starter and baking traditional (and time-consuming) artisanal breads, jump on the no-knead phenomenon, or simply try your hand at a quick bread, feeling the dough in your hands, cutting into a warm loaf, and slathering a thick slice with butter is unlike anything else I can imagine. If the from-scratch approach is a bit too much for you, make sure you buy decent stuff—the kind of loaves you find festooned with a halo of flour and slashes across the crust—and you'll be tickled at how happy it makes your company and how much easier it makes filling out the table.

I may be the exception in these days of gluten-shunning, but the first thing I do when I visit our cottage on the weekends is pull half a loaf of bread out of the freezer to thaw. I make the bread (from Chad Robertson's *Tartine Bread*) in batches of four loaves every other month or so, and the two of us can handily finish half a loaf over the course of a weekend. From toast in the morning, sandwiches at lunch, and a wedge at dinner, bread never sticks around long in our house. This is true of crackers, grissini (breadsticks), and those addictive Italian snacks called taralli, too. Homemade or store-bought, these all have an important spot on the grazing table.

the usefulness of a good tomato (and other near-naked dishes)

As I write this, it's early September and the tomatoes are within minutes of being past their peak. Right now, they are perfect, misshapen orbs—stunning in scarlet, honeyed yellow, the preternaturally striped lime green known as a Zebra, and all shades in between. Absurdly juicy, they seem to weep before the knife even breaks their skin, and the flavors (because every kind does seem to have its own) are beyond any words I'm familiar with; none of the usual suspects—sweet, tangy, acidic, sublime—do justice.

They're also, to my mind, one of the most practical and utilitarian ingredients in the fruit bowl (though the avocado is a close second). Growing up in California, my sister and I were regularly sent off to school, our brown bag lunches packed not with the ubiquitous apple or orange, but with a tomato and a small plastic baggie of salt. Sitting on the playground, we would eat the tomatoes whole, tearing ever so slightly at the corner of the top-knotted baggie to create a makeshift saltshaker, the best way to add a sprinkle with each bite.

Like summer itself, good tomatoes' days are numbered, but while they're around, they are perfect foil for a breakfast egg—scrambled, poached, or otherwise; unrivaled at lunch laid over avocado or soft cheese on toast; and come dinner, they can be chopped and tossed with almost anything in-season (basil, peaches, cucumbers, corn . . . seriously, *anything*). Whether simply sliced and laid in a dish next to other naked or barely-touched ingredients in midsummer, or slow-roasted and swimming in buttery olive oil come winter, the tomato's usefulness in the grazing kitchen can't be overstated. While available, a good tomato is the cook's stalwart companion; it makes everything better and demands so little.

Other fresh ingredients may not demonstrate quite the same full-spectrum utilitarianism, but many do serve a similar purpose. An avocado, a plate of fresh figs or radishes, a quick-pickled red onion, a sliced cucumber set aside a dish of yogurt spiked with dill, a dish of sweet corn stripped off the cob and sprinkled with lime juice and salt—all of these are essential to the grazing table and, when taken together, can even make up an entire meal—what Ken calls The Sliced Lunch. When all you have to do is pull out various meats, cheeses, vegetables, crackers or bread, and a tomato, you have a sliced lunch—and how perfect is a meal where you need nothing more than a sharp knife or a pat of butter on the table?

cheese and making friends
with your monger

As someone who cooks for a living, I'm about to make a slightly embarrassing confession: I used to be scared of the cheese counter. Or, more accurately, intimidated by the wealth of cheese behind said counter. Yes, I've tangled with homemade tagliatelle and faced off with offal, but in front of those different and carefully crafted curds, I was overwhelmed. Not because I don't love cheese with a deep and unwavering passion, but because, like wine, there just always seemed so much to know—or so much I didn't know. But because I adore cheese in almost all of its forms, and because it's a critical element in the grazing kitchen, I set out to rid myself of my anxiety in the only way I knew how: I tasted a lot of cheese.

I also got a quick lesson from a cheesemonger friend who helped me navigate my education. One of the most useful things she told me is that European cheese names encompass a broad array of eating experiences, while American cheeses have one name for each cheese. Meaning, you may like Manchego, but what you've enjoyed could have been a young, aged, or even an oil-cured version—ostensibly three different cheeses. Same goes for Brie, cheddar, or Stilton. European cheeses may come from the same region, bear the same name, and illustrate similar characteristics, but they can vary wildly in terms of taste and texture. All of which makes it slightly confusing for the burgeoning cheese lover.

On the other hand, American cheeses are individually identified by the maker along with a unique name; meaning, if you fall in love with a specific American cheese (for instance, Cowgirl Creamery's Mt. Tam or Cato Corner's Hooligan), rest assured that you'll be getting the same cheese time and again (barring any major changes to the process by the cheese maker or seasonal variations). This was an *aha* moment for me, especially with such an enticing array of artisanal farmstead cheeses now being produced right here at home.

Of course it all gets more complicated as you talk about the families of cheese (fresh, bloomy rind, washed rind, etc.) and the different types of milk (cow, sheep, goat), but for someone like me, an academic explanation wasn't what I was looking for; I needed the sensory experience to understand it, and I don't think I'm alone. The only way I know how to be comfy at the cheese counter is to find one with a kind and patient cheesemonger who will let you try a bit of this and taste a bit of that before you buy. Good cheese is expensive, so it's worth taking that deep breath and asking for a nibble rather than ending up with a hunk of bunk you don't enjoy. In my experience, you also don't need to walk away having purchased three or four cheeses all designed to complement one another on a board. Of course, I love a good cheese board as much as the next girl, but spending a bit of money on one really nice cheese is smarter than picking up two or three that are just okay and discovering them a few weeks later, furry and green, huddled at the back of the fridge.

it's because of the pig

Years ago I asked my therapist if she was a vegetarian. It's a funny question to ask your therapist, I suppose, but I was desperate to know anything at all about her; she was the most frustrating of clinicians, the one who knows everything about you but shares virtually nothing of her own life. So one day, as slyly as I could, I asked about her eating habits—specifically if she was meat-free. I was startled to receive not just an answer (she dodged pretty much every other personal question I'd ever posed), but a very direct one: "I would be," she said, "But I love the pig." With those short utterances, suddenly I knew a lot more about this woman to whom I had bared all my deepest secrets. I knew we had something in common as well, something that went beyond our therapist-patient relationship. We both loved the pig and yet neither of us was fully comfortable with eating animals. It was a conundrum that couldn't be sorted, a hypocrisy that couldn't be ignored. We simply had to accept it (largely what therapy is for, to help us accept what we cannot change).

And I guess I have. Because while I love animals more than I love most people, and I could give up the odd grilled steak or braised short rib without *too* much complaint, it's my passion for the pig, and really all cured meats, that keeps me a carnivore. Coppa, prosciutto, *jamón serrano* and *ibérico*, soppressata, guanciale, pancetta, speck, and bresaola—they're my downfall. And one of the main reasons I'm such a devotee of grazing.

While I'm definitely a meat eater (guilty conscience here on full display), I should say that Ken and I don't actually consume that much of it. We might share a small steak on a Friday night and we do like to roast a chicken on Saturdays—one small bird gets us dinner plus lots of leftovers, and keeps us well stocked with stock—but mostly we use small amounts of whatever cured meats we have on hand to fill out a meal; not so little as to be garnish, but not so much as to be considered the focal point of the table. Especially with good-quality charcuterie, you don't need a lot of it to satiate your desire. The intensity of the flavors—the buttery sweetness of aged prosciutto, the musty smokiness of a cabernet-colored bresaola, or the spiced, fatty bite of a powdery skinned soppressata—all of these have enough distinct character and robustness of

flavor to warrant being served in small portions. And that's just what you want to do when you're filling the table with lots of other wonderful things.

If you tend to be partial to prosciutto or are stuck solely on soppressata, the one suggestion I have is to venture further afield. Charcuterie is a lot like cheese—you need to taste it to know if you like it, but there's a lot out there to discover. If you can, find yourself a good Italian deli or a decent specialty store (worst case, jump online) and then be brave: Try a rustic *finocchiona*, a fennel-infused Tuscan salami (said to have been created when a boy stole a salami and ran into a field of wild fennel to savor his purloined snack); dare to try *caccicatori*, a dried sausage made from ground pork and supposedly carried in the pockets of hunters for sustenance in days of yore; or if you're feeling indulgent, savor a few slices of *jamón ibérico de Bellota*, a buttery, fat-slicked sweet ham made from black-hoofed, acorn-eating pigs raised in the oak forests between Spain and Portugal. Yes, some of these will be more expensive and harder to find, but you don't need to buy too much or go all-out all the time. Some days, a slice of salami and a hunk of cheese—no matter what their pedigree or fanciful history—work just fine.

selective snobbery and some shortcuts i can live with

Most any of my friends will tell you that I'm a bit batty when it comes to homemade anything. I make 90 percent of the bread we eat, croissants too; our granola is from scratch, and I rarely buy packaged cookies unless we're really in a pinch (but yeah, it happens to the best of us). You'll never catch me with a tub of packaged salsa in my fridge, no bottled salad dressing will cross my threshold, there's no chance of a frozen pizza in our house, and a can of sodium-laced soup? No way. All that said . . .

I couldn't live without canned tomatoes, beans, and sardines. I love the simplicity of smoked salmon and the convenience of naturally cured mackerel and trout that come hermetically sealed from the refrigerated section. I have no problem with a jar of imported tuna (the kind that comes preserved in olive oil), pepperoncini, anchovies, artichokes, and sun-dried tomatoes. I can be counted on to have a box of peas in my freezer at all times, maybe even a bag of frozen peaches or berries too, and a bag of corn or a box of spinach is totally acceptable as well. Come winter, those plastic tubs of arugula and baby lettuce are a no-brainer; they're just in better shape most of the time than the rubber band–bound heads of lettuce stacked and squashed together in the produce section. Sure, I like to make homemade pasta now and then, but the dried stuff is my go-to on a weekly basis. And here it is, my deepest darkest secret revealed: I love Cape Cod Sea Salt potato chips. They're my kryptonite, my drug of choice, and I'm a full-on addict.

These are my shortcuts, cheats, timesaving tricks, and guilty (packaged) pleasures. And I am totally okay with all of them. I know there are those who will judge me on all fronts, but I've come to terms with these shortcuts and have no regrets. Whether you cook a lot or a little, I promise you will have yours too—we all do. And we don't have to agree on what they are. If you're okay with chicken stock from a box or pre-grated cheese, I could try to convince you otherwise, but then you might try to take away my pre-washed lettuce or worse, my chips, and that would break my heart.

It's not about proving who can do more work in the kitchen; it's about doing as much as you can to feel good about what you're cooking, while still enjoying the process. If you're on the fence about any of your peccadillos, the barometer I use is the old Michael Pollan adage: If it has more than five ingredients or you can't pronounce it, don't eat it. (Cape Cod Sea Salt potato chips have only three ingredients, by the way.)

leftovers as inspiration

A huge part of my job as a food stylist is shopping, and I'm pretty good at it. The part I'm not as skilled at is throwing away what's left over at the end of a shoot. Most of the leftovers get divvied up amongst the crew when we finish, but there's always that lump of Parmesan, half bag of wild rice, handful of cherry tomatoes, or pound of sausage that no one grabbed. And I can't bear to toss it out. So I bring it home and try to make use of it as best I can. I realize this isn't an experience most home cooks will share with me—getting stuck with bits and pieces of fresh food at the end of a long day—but we all have leftovers that we can put to great use if we think about it, especially when we're conceiving smaller plates.

Leftovers can stare back at us from their shelf in the fridge, shaming us into eating them before they go bad, but I like to think of them as a starting point for something else entirely: inspiration for a new meal, rather than the scraps of a previous one. Yes, the shredded chicken left over from Sunday's roast is easily savored on a slice of toast for lunch, but it can also become the basis for individual chicken pot pies—ramekins filled with ample vegetables, a gentle rosemary-infused sauce, and a quick flaky crust. A leftover cup of risotto can certainly be reheated for a solo lunch, but when rolled into balls, dredged in breadcrumbs, and fried until golden brown, it becomes the start of a perfectly unplanned grazing meal.

In our house, tomatoes that start going soft get swaddled in plastic bags for the freezer and ultimately turned into sauce; heels of bread are also frozen, nestled together in a bag to later become homemade breadcrumbs; small pieces of meat and those few bits of roasted vegetables that didn't get eaten all get frozen for a second chance at becoming something on the grazing table. Even if you don't have the energy or inclination to turn a bit of leftover shrimp into a spring roll or a cup of sautéed mushrooms into an individual quiche, you can still use these delicious odds and ends in their simplest form the next day.

Every so often, usually after a holiday or a dinner party, we find ourselves with a fridge full of sundries, so we have our favorite kind of grazing meal—the kind where containers of all sizes are pulled out, paper-wrapped bits and plastic-enveloped pieces are strewn across the counter, and what was last night's fête becomes this evening's feast. The last slab of slow-cooked pork gets cut into slices, those few remaining stems of sautéed broccoli rabe are drizzled with lush olive oil and sprinkled with Parmesan cheese, and a pint of pureed butternut squash is gently reheated and served with that last half of baguette for dipping. It's not unlike the all-American tradition of the day after Thanksgiving—turning the remains of one night's dinner into another meal entirely, reminiscent yet remarkable in its own right. This is grazing in perhaps its purest form— making the most of what's right in front of us without having to do much cooking at all.

what to sip while grazing

I like to drink and do so daily. I'm not one of those weekday teetotalers who lets loose come Friday night; rather, I look forward to my glass of wine most days. Like dinner itself, the ritual of a post-workday tipple is something that makes the rest of it all worthwhile. I also have no problem with drinking alone. Let the neighbors talk— sometimes after a long day, walking into a quiet house, starting to cook, and pouring myself a glass of wine to sip silently with nothing more than the hum of the fridge or the purr of the cat as background music is better than yoga (or at least, on par).

I also don't subscribe to the thinking that white goes with some things and red with others, or that certain wines fit specific seasons. Why save a refreshing rosé for summer or resist a gutsy red in mid-August if that's what your heart desires? What you drink (be it wine, beer, or a cocktail) just needs to be something you'll enjoy as much as the food you're making. Sometimes nothing satisfies my thirst like a cold beer, whether alongside a plate of oysters or a burger and fries. Other times, no matter what's on the menu, a proper cocktail is what I'll crave, the ritual of making the drink almost as mellowing as the elixir itself. It doesn't matter what the experts say or what the calendar reads—when it comes to choosing a drink, it's really a matter of personal preference.

Deciding what to pull out of the wine fridge after a long day usually gets the same amount of attention as the meal I'm cooking. Meaning that on nights when I'm stretching dough for an easy pizza or boiling water for a simple bowl of pasta, I want to grab one of our house wines, those more-than-serviceable, readily drinkable, totally affordable bottles that we buy by the case so there's always something decent on hand. We call these our "pizza wines" because while they're good, they're not so fussy or fancy that they can't be served with a slice. These are our day-to-day dinner wines, and it's nice to find a few that you like and can buy with confidence and regularity. Like good cheese, you want to experiment with wine and find ones you really like and can buy again and again, but you don't want to have to taste a lot of plonk along the way. Take the time to start a conversation with your local wine merchant; at first, it can be tough trying to articulate what you like (it can be awkward talking to an expert in oenology), but letting someone with expertise offer some guidance can save you a lot of half-finished bottles and wasted money.

Beyond our workday wines, we also have those that we save for weekends, whether friends or family come around or we simply want to mix it up. These are usually more adventurous bottles than our old standbys, and this is where Ken comes in. He can spend an hour or more wandering the aisles of the wine store, reading about and contemplating new wines for us to try (he can also get lost in Home Depot this way, looking at lumber or pondering over power tools, both habits becoming worrisome at times). We'll often spend a bit more on the sleek French whites I adore and luscious California reds he fancies—wines we are sure to let breathe for a bit (how often do I open a bottle after a long day and not even think to give it some air?), bottles we make the effort to sip more slowly, to drink with some awareness and appreciation. None of which is to say that these wines can't be enjoyed Monday through Friday if the mood arises, but just that when life slows down a bit, it's nice to acknowledge the moment with a thoughtful sip.

In general, our favorites wines (not being true collectors or connoisseurs) tend to be French whites from Burgundy and the Loire Valley (think Chablis, Pouilly-Fuissé, Sancerre, and Pouilly-Fumé); Italian wines from Alto Adige, Friuli, Abruzzo, and Tuscany; Albariños and Riojas from Spain; many of the New World Sauvignon Blancs from Australia and New Zealand; and of course the Zinfandels, Pinot Noirs, Petite Sirahs, and Ken's coveted Cabernets from California and Oregon. All of these wines sit happily on the table with a smattering of small plates, but so will your favorites. In my mind, drinking is just like eating—only you know what you like, and that's exactly what you should serve.

grazing menus
(from simple spreads to full-on soirées)

Nothing in this book is hard to make. Some things are sparingly simple, while others take a little time and a bit of effort (but not much, really). What is most challenging about the concept of grazing is putting together a menu that feels cohesive and has a sensibility. The more difficult aspect is creating a continuous thread of flavors and textures that allows the eaters to weave their way from one dish to the next, to travel fluidly from plate to plate with a sense of intent. To help you begin unearthing the logic of a well-laid grazing table, here are some of my menus. You'll notice some recipes found in this book, of course, but you'll also see single ingredient suggestions for filling out the table, thoughts on adding cheese or charcuterie, and ideas for including fruit or sliced vegetables for a more robust showing. This is where the pantry becomes vital and your creativity as a shopper comes into focus.

TRANSPORTING TAPAS
A plate of *jamón*

A dish of green olives

Blistered Shishito Peppers with Flaky Salt (*page 73*)

Spanish Tortilla with Sweet Onion and Thyme (*page 120*)

Pan con Tomate (*page 43*)

A DOG DAYS LUNCH
Melon Soup with Prosciutto Shards (*page 34*)

Persian Cucumbers, Snap Peas, and Red Onion with Lemon Zest (*page 53*)

Flaky Cheddar Biscuits with Heirloom Tomatoes and Peaches (*page 113*)

A bowl of cherries

ODE TO SPRING AND ALL THINGS GREEN
A good loaf of bread with salty butter

Parmesan Pea Spread (*page 41*)

Asparagus and Herb Frittata Bites (*page 130*)

Zucchini Ribbons with Herbed Goat Cheese (*page 55*)

A FRENCH AFFAIR FOR MANY
A good baguette

Radishes with Blue Butter (*page 5*)

Herb-Scented Gougères (*page 118*)

Ham and Cornichons on Buttered Baguette (*page 45*)

Creamy Chicken Liver Pâté with (or without) Red Onion and Raspberry Jam on Brioche (*page 114*)

A Trio of Tartlettes (*page 123*)

Potato and Leek Soup (*page 88*), served chilled a la vichyssoise

A (NEARLY) SPONTANEOUS SUNDAY SOIRÉE
Smoked Trout–Stuffed Deviled Eggs (*page 26*)

Pea Shooters with Parmesan Crisps (*page 87*)

A plate of smoked salmon speckled with capers

Lemon-Tarragon Chicken Skewers (*page 106*)

Eiffel Tower–Inspired Coconut Macaroons (*page 177*)

just shopping

We all have our bad habits. I am notorious for snacking while I cook. It can be a vellum-thin slice of prosciutto, a wedge of briny artichoke, a mouthful of grated Parmesan, or a handful of chickpeas—I'm not fussy. I just love to taste as I go. It's a weakness for sure, but also a perk of being the cook, or in this case, the shopper. Some of my favorite covert bites—those stolen corners of cheese and purloined pieces of cucumber—are little more than well-chosen ingredients made pretty on a plate, exactly what you'll find here. These are not recipes, so please don't be misled; rather, they are ideas for good things that go with other good things—that's all.

an unconventional plate of vegetables

CRUDITÉS HAVE NEVER BEEN MY THING. IT'S NOT because I don't adore raw vegetables—it's just that the ubiquitous carrot sticks, broccoli florets, and red pepper slices fall a bit flat next to a platter of unctuous cheeses or a dish of nectarous olives. I know people say they like crudités, but could it really be the creamy dip they adore, the hummus or guacamole, that keeps them reaching for another celery stick? I always figured that was the real attraction, until it dawned on me that the raw vegetables I like the most aren't commonly served as crudités. This hit me one night while I was cooking dinner, when Ken turned to me and said, "You're eating all the sprouts." He was right. We eat roasted Brussels sprouts like they're going out of style in the winter, but while they're sitting on the baking sheet, glistening with oil and sparkling with flaky salt awaiting their turn in the oven, I snack on them mercilessly. The oil and salt tenderize the papery outer leaves and soften their cruciferous bite, making them irresistible—the perfect raw vegetable for premeal munching.

And there it was: With that subtle scolding, I had an epiphany. It wasn't crudités I found lacking, but the array of crudités set before me. I love fennel slices so thin they flutter on your tongue, crisp sugar snap peas, and peppery radishes. Those young rainbow-colored carrots can work, or more mature ones turned into curls with the whip of a peeler. Even just tweaking the way vegetables are sliced makes a difference in how they appear on the plate, appeal to the senses, and sit on the tongue, which is why for me, a few sprouts gleaming with oil or a cucumber curl win out over another grape tomato or celery stick any day.

recipe continues

an unconventional plate of vegetables

Brussels sprouts

Extra-virgin olive oil

Sea salt

Persian (mini) cucumbers

Asparagus

Fennel

Rainbow radishes

French breakfast radishes or other small red radishes

Young carrots (rainbow are fun)

Sugar snap peas

Baby squash

Baby cauliflower

Treviso, endive, or other lettuce leaves

Trim the Brussels sprouts and halve them. Toss them in a bowl with a nice coating of olive oil and use your hands to massage the oil into the sprouts. Sprinkle them with sea salt and set aside.

Meanwhile, use a vegetable peeler to slice the cucumbers lengthwise into long thin ribbons. Cut the asparagus spears in half lengthwise. Use a mandoline or sharp knife to shave the fennel into thin pieces, being sure to leave them slightly intact at the root end.

Peel and cut the rainbow radish into thin disks. Trim the breakfast radishes, leaving just an inch or so of green at the top. If you can only find red radishes, use the coarse side of a scrub sponge to scrub the radishes gently around their middles to reveal a bit of the white underneath.

Peel the carrots and trim the tops so that less than an inch of green remains. Snip the ends off the snap peas if they need it.

Place the lightly marinated Brussels sprouts and all the other cleaned and cut vegetables on a platter and cluster tightly together. Serve with a small bowl of olive oil and sea salt for dipping.

radishes with blue butter

BLUE BUTTER MAY CHANGE YOUR LIFE. IT'S ONE OF THOSE absurdly easy kitchen tricks that—assuming you like blue cheese—make almost everything better. Spread it on toast, top a steak with a slab, or smear it on any vegetable—raw or cooked—that you please. The only really important thing to know, beyond its life-changing qualities, is to use good blue cheese. My knees go weak for a hunk of Stilton, so that's what I choose, but if your favorite is Roquefort or Cabrales, feel free. The idea here is to simply add that sharp, salty, and, yes, stinky essence to the peppery flavor of the radishes for something a wee bit gutsier than the classic preparation usually served with butter and salt. *See photograph on page 16.*

½ stick (4 tablespoons) unsalted butter, at room temperature

2 ounces Stilton or other good-quality blue cheese, at room temperature

12–16 French breakfast radishes or other small radishes, halved

Flaky sea salt

In a bowl, mash the butter and cheese together with a fork until well combined. Transfer to a serving dish and serve with radishes and flaky salt. Or anything you can think of to smear it on, really.

quintessential all-shopping, light-chopping antipasti

I THINK THAT ALL COOKS, WHETHER WE ADMIT IT OR NOT, want to be loved for our food. Even the most humble among us—those who are demure and deflect all compliments, even those of us with kitchen modesty built into our DNA—can't help but feel a warm blush when people like what we've made. So it can be a bit of a heartbreaker to put out a lovingly prepared tray of snacks—to hear the oohs-and-ahs, to see the wedges of cheese vanish, the slivers of charcuterie disappear, and the marinated vegetables recede into the waiting mouths of friends—believing that as a cook, you weren't really responsible for this crowd-pleaser, that it wasn't your nuanced seasoning or precise searing that brought this beauty into being. You were of course the clever shopper, gifted chopper, and the one with an eye for layering, clustering, and arranging, but still, it was all so easy, such a cheat really, that you feel like a heel accepting the praise. To this I say (and I'm talking to myself here too): Stop with the self-deprecation. It may be the simplest of ways to dazzle but it still counts; shopping and choosing and slicing and spreading is not mindless at all, and while it may not require the skill of knowing rare from medium or soft-boiled from hard, it takes imagination to do it well.

Stay simple and stick with the suggestions below, or get more extravagant if you must—roast your own tomatoes (page 64) instead of buying sun-dried; grill thin slices of eggplant or zucchini, drizzle them with olive oil, and dapple them with fresh oregano; add a dish of cornichons, Marcona almonds, sliced figs, pears, or melon. The key to the perfect antipasti is using the best ingredients you can rationalize, keeping it bountiful but not cluttered, and being okay with saying, "Thanks, I'm so glad you like it. It was all me."

My Marinated Beans (page 25)	Oil-packed marinated sun-dried tomatoes	Ball of burrata or dish of small mozzarella balls
Long-stemmed, marinated artichokes	Cured meat (soppressata, prosciutto, coppa, bresaola, or better, a mix)	Pepperoncini
Cerignola, Sevillano, Castelvetrano, or other brine-soaked olives	Hunk of Parmesan or other hard cheese	Roasted peppers
		Breadsticks, crackers, or toasts

Gather everything together and arrange on a platter or multiple plates so that contrasting colors and textures live next to one another. That's it. Really.

sardines on crackers with lemon and thyme

IF MY FONDNESS FOR GRAZING COMES FROM anywhere, it's almost certainly from the weekend lunches we used to have as kids. My parents were early adopters of the fixer-upper and, as such, weekends at our house were spent in constant construction mode. For the Lenzers, a normal Saturday meant stripping French windows or laying sprinkler systems, none of which lent itself to leisurely meals by the pool. Meaning lunch was always sort of an afterthought. In my memory, it was only after my sister and I had voiced long and loud our desire to eat that my parents would give in and head to the kitchen. There we'd pull salami, cheese, crackers, and maybe some liverwurst from the fridge and lay it on the old country-style table that served as a center island. Sometimes, at my dad's instigation, there would be small bowls of borscht topped with sour cream. All of this was good, but the best of these ramshackle family lunches was when the sardines came out. Shiny tins opened with a key revealed perfectly packed and wonderfully oily fish that my dad meticulously layered on Triscuit crackers and garnished with nothing more than a squeeze of lemon.

I don't keep Triscuits in the house these days (I'm partial to chips when I want that salty fix), but when I'm working at home and need lunch, I can regularly be counted on to stand in the kitchen with a can of sardines in hand, half a lemon lying on the counter, and a few crackers if I've got them. I tell myself these omega-3-loaded treats are good for my skin, but in truth, there are few lunches quite as satisfying.

2 cans (3.75 ounces each) oil-packed sardines	**12–16 Triscuits or your favorite crackers**	**2–3 sprigs fresh thyme, leaves picked**
	1–2 lemons	

Gently remove the sardines from their containers and place on a cutting board. Cut each sardine into thirds (don't worry if they crumble a bit) and transfer a piece to a cracker. Repeat with all the sardines and all the crackers. Squeeze fresh lemon over all and sprinkle with thyme leaves.

preserved lemon and herb marinated olives

IF YOU EVER PLAN TO COME TO MY HOUSE TO EAT, there's something you should know about me: I'm a bit of a one-trick pony. I wonder if this is true of all cooks, or if I'm just abnormally stuck in my ways. Or maybe it's because my job requires me to cook different things every day—when left to my own devices, I fall back on old favorites with such comfort and ease. Take my preserved lemons, for example. I've been making these for years now and I can't help but put them on and in as many things as possible. Sure, I could come up with another way to add that elusive sweet-salty-citric bite, but I don't. I just keep going back and making more preserved lemons; they really just make everything better. Especially olives. I love olives. From the time I was a kid and discovered the wonder of sticking those inky-colored, metallic-flavored canned olives on every finger, to the creamy, thick-fleshed Sevillano giants I first tasted in southern Spain, I've rarely encountered an olive I don't like. But if you're shopping at a grocery store and not an Italian delicatessen or specialty store, you'll find that the olives often need a little oomph. That's where the preserved lemons come in. If you've got these in your fridge already, it's a no-brainer; a dalliance between preserved lemons and olives with a few fresh herbs tossed in for good measure turns the ubiquitous into the revelatory.

2 cups brine-cured olives

½ cup chopped preserved lemons, homemade (page 22) or store-bought, plus more as needed

1 cup extra-virgin olive oil

1–2 sprigs fresh oregano, leaves picked and chopped

1 sprig fresh rosemary, leaves picked and chopped

2–3 sprigs fresh thyme, leaves picked

1 teaspoon red chili flakes

Sea salt

In a large jar, combine the olives, preserved lemons, olive oil, herbs, and chili flakes and mix well. Taste the marinade and decide if you want to add more lemons or some salt, and adjust as needed. Let the olives stand in the fridge for at least a couple of hours or up to a week. To serve, bring to room temperature and spoon into small bowls or serve right out of the jar.

fresh figs with serrano ham

FIGS ARE MY WEAKNESS. WELL, I HAVE MANY, BUT FIGS are pretty high on the list. When I'm home alone and it's time for lunch, a generous nub of cheese and a handful of figs is pretty standard fare. Halved over yogurt and my homemade granola (page 181), they flesh out a winsome breakfast. Then there's that almond cake I adore (page 161), where figs are featured prominently when I have my way. (Ken is partial to substituting blueberries or rhubarb and raspberries, but sometimes I'm able to persuade him.) Unlike other fruits, figs have the capacity to sweep me off to somewhere more exotic, where warm spices cloud the air and richly colored carpets line the halls of dark, cool rooms. With their inky-toned skin, often blushing green right at the stem, and honeyed flavor paired with a gentle crunch, figs are seductive. If you've had a rough day, wrap a few figs in wisps of Serrano ham, pour a glass of wine, and put on some music. Madeline Peyroux or Melody Gardot are good choices, while sometimes Roxy Music or Joni Mitchell better fit the mood; and every now and then, nothing is better than Kate Bush and her ethereal siren-like voice. Then sit on the floor. Better yet, lie down on the floor and stare up at the ceiling for a few minutes. If someone walks in, they may wonder, but it works, I swear. *See an additional photograph on page xiii.*

| 12 fresh figs | 6 slices Serrano ham or other dry-cured ham | Balsamic vinegar, for drizzling (optional) |

Slice each fig in half lengthwise. Tear each piece of ham in half as well. Wrap each fig half in a band of the ham if you like, or simply serve the figs on a plate with the ham and let guests assemble as they choose. Drizzle with balsamic vinegar, if desired.

cherries with cheese and pistachios

WHEN I WAS IN COLLEGE, I HAD WHAT WOULD NOW BE called a "girl crush" on a friend of mine named Cybele. She was a couple of years older, had a short auburn bob, wore slim capris with ballet flats (there might even have been a scarf tied at the neck from time to time), read Doris Lessing and Margaret Atwood, and carried herself with a sense of sophistication I found intoxicating. Needless to say, I was thrilled when she and her girlfriend Renee invited me over for a glass of wine one afternoon. Their living room had a bohemian style to it that I immediately adored; Mexican blankets were tossed over old squishy chairs, batik and velvet pillows lay scattered on the floor, Joan Armatrading belted from the stereo, and Cybele poured a deeply red wine into oversized green goblets while wearing a vibrant caftan that seemed to spill like the wine itself over her shoulders and pool at her ankles in bursts of claret and gold. There was a board laden with fruit, cheeses, and nuts on the coffee table. My guess, all these years later, is that the cheeses included a waxy Brie and a few slices of block cheddar, the fruit was likely grapes, and the nuts, well I'm going to go with canned and mixed. But at the time, all I could think was, "This is perfect." Granted, it sounds terrifically pretentious in hindsight, but back then I was besotted by it all. No, I could never wear a caftan and take myself seriously, and the days of pillows on the floor being a thing are gone for me (I like a tidy house). But I still love Joan Armatrading, read Lessing and Atwood when the mood strikes, and while I've long lost track of Cybele, always think of her and smile when I lay out a spread of fruit and cheese.

recipe continues

cherries with cheese and pistachios

| 1 pound cherries (don't bother to stem or pit) | 1 cup pistachios (with the shell on; half the fun is prying them open) | Cheese (whatever you love most) |

It's as simple as it sounds: Put the cherries in one bowl and the pistachios in another. Be sure the cheese is at room temperature and place it on a board with a knife. Enjoy.

Some ideas on cheese: *If you're trying to break away from the Brie wheel and goat cheese log, here are some thoughts. With cherries or other stone fruit, I like something creamy, like Three Sisters from Nettle Meadow Farm: It's a soft, bloomy rind cheese made of sheep, goat, and cow's milk. For something equally as decadent but a little more lemony, try their Kunik triple crème made from goat and Jersey cow's milk. And if you're lucky enough to stumble upon it, Gubbeen, a semi-soft cow's milk cheese from County Cork, Ireland, is a treat. A bit nutty and a little earthy, it's worth looking out for.*

If you're doing a fruit and cheese plate with autumnal fruit like apples, pears, and figs, my mind wanders to a nosey blue like Stilton. If that's not your thing, try a sheep's milk cheese from the Basque country, like P'tit Basque or Ossau-Iraty. Both of these are nutty, sweet, and surprisingly creamy for semi-hard cheeses. If you like truly hard Alpine-style cheese, Consider Bardwell in Vermont has Rupert, an aged Jersey cow's milk cheese that's both bright and sharp (but my favorite of theirs, the one I can eat by the wedge alone in the kitchen and call it lunch, is Pawlet, a creamy Italian-style toma like no other).

Keep in mind that while one really good cheese is totally fine (I find setting out one favorite gives people a chance to really focus and taste the nuances of the cheese), it's also nice to offer a mix. Try setting out hard and soft cheeses so there's a play of textures as well as flavors—and make sure each cheese gets its own knife, too.

charcuterie-draped grissini

THERE ARE THINGS I INSIST ON MAKING FROM SCRATCH: pizza dough, granola, salad dressing, and pesto sauce. Then there are things I prefer to make from scratch but feel okay buying when it's a decent store-bought version: bread, croissants, pasta, and crackers. Grissini, the long skinny breadsticks that rival potato chips for best crunchy snack of all time, also fall into that second category. I like making my own, and when I have the time, I do. But I also believe that there's a limit to what home cooks need to make from scratch in order to feel okay about themselves. There are fabulous packaged grissini out there (the best ones are very thin and made in Italy), and I almost always have a box in the pantry so that these silly little snacks can be made in mere minutes. If you have an Italian specialty store near you, look there first; happily, more and more grocery stores are stocking nice ones, too. *See photograph on next page.*

32 grissini

16 thin slices soppressata, prosciutto, coppa, bresaola, or other cured meat

Roll 2 grissini together with a single slice of cured meat. If you're using soppressata or bresaola, you will want to serve them lying on a plate, but if you're using prosciutto or coppa, which are stickier, you can serve them standing up in a mason jar or glass.

FOLLOWING PAGE: *Radishes with Blue Butter* (PAGE 5) | *My Marinated Beans* (PAGE 25) | *Charcuterie-Draped Grissini* | *Prosciutto, Asparagus, and Arugula Rolls* (PAGE 29)

oysters with bubbly mignonette

I ONCE READ A BOOK CALLED *THE OYSTERS OF Locmariaquer* by Eleanor Clark. It's the story of a town in Brittany devoted to the cultivation of the Belon oyster, also called *les plates* or the "the flat ones." The proprietor of my neighborhood bookshop, a mouse hole of a place called Three Lives, recommended the book to me. The ownership has changed over now, but it used to be owned by two women, Jill and Jenny, both of whom had a genius for curating the best selection of books and somehow knowing exactly what you needed to read at that moment to change your life. For some reason, on one particular day, Jill decided I needed to know about Belon oysters. Go figure. Having burrowed down under the covers that night and lost myself to the land of briny bivalves, I became fixated on the idea of eating a tray of these mollusks while sipping a glass of flinty Chablis and staring out at the steely English Channel. I decided then and there that on one of my birthdays—it didn't matter which—I would make this happen. Here's the thing: It hasn't happened yet. I haven't given up (ideally, I have a lot of birthdays left for this literary-inspired fantasy to become reality), but as I bide my time, I've come up with a satisfactory facsimile of the experience. The oysters aren't necessarily from Belon, the Chablis is most likely the remains of whatever we opened last night, and the view of the English Channel is certainly lacking, but otherwise it's exactly the same.

1 shallot, finely minced	**Freshly ground black pepper**	**2–3 tablespoons Prosecco or other bubbly dry wine**
¼ cup sherry vinegar	**12 or more oysters**	

In a small bowl, combine the shallot, vinegar, and a generous amount of pepper. Let sit while you shuck the oysters.

To shuck the oysters, use a safety glove. For years I didn't, and I have the scars to prove it. If you really aren't going to bother, at least hold the oyster in a dry kitchen towel as you insert the tip of the shucking knife into the little hinge at the corner of the oyster. Twist the knife into the hinge as best you can and lift upward to loosen the top shell from the bottom. Some oysters are easier to open than others, but ideally once the knife makes its way between the shells, you can pry them apart; try to keep the lower shell upright as you do so to save as much of the briny liquor as possible.

When all the oysters have been shucked, transfer them to a plate of crushed ice. Put the mignonette into a small serving bowl and top with a couple tablespoons of Prosecco. Serve with the remaining Prosecco (of course).

mostly chopping

Plates brimming with vegetables bathed in zesty vinaigrettes; simple spreads meant to be slathered on charred toast; bowls filled with chilled summer soups; dishes replete with tangy beans, smoky deviled eggs, or sushi-grade tuna laid nearly bare—these are the foods that entice me, the kind that can be eaten with fingers or shared from a communal platter. The ingredients need only a nudge from the cook: a bit of oil and a sprinkle of salt definitely, maybe a smashed clove of garlic or a mashed-up anchovy, possibly a drizzle of syrup or a squirt of citrus, even a showering of tender or resinous herbs. They take a little bit of work, but not a lot; some can be done in less than 5 minutes, and others can be made well in advance. Choose one, maybe two, add some well-curated, store-bought bits and pieces, and call it a day.

preserved lemons

RIGHT NOW, IN OUR TINY LIVING ROOM IN Connecticut, we have two Mexican lime plants, one Meyer lemon tree, a Key lime tree, and a kumquat tree. All are small enough to fit in pots and stay that way to make the seasonal sojourn inside when the East Coast begins to chill.

Our obsession with growing our own citrus in a climate that is decidedly adverse to our plans may seem futile, but it's a challenge I find comforting. Two Meyer lemons a year, eight kumquats . . . those aren't yields to brag about, yet each brightly flavored orb gives us a sense of delight—it's been created against the odds of Mother Nature, in spite of the obstacles she throws in front of us in the form of freezing temperatures and inches of snow. This soulful battle we wage makes me feel in touch with the elements and at one with a higher power, but the truth is this: Because our bounty is so meager, we rely on care packages from my mom and dad's garden in Los Angeles—flat-rate boxes crammed with fruit (the Mexican limes, calamansi, Meyer lemons, and sour oranges that grow like weeds out west)—to keep us well stocked. The Mexican limes are the most prolific and astounding—and when thinly sliced and preserved in shallots, garlic, sugar, and salt, they become a Moroccan treat. The key is the thin skin (less bitter pith), which is why, if you don't have access to a tree in California, Meyer lemons or small organic lemons are usually your best bet when making this recipe.

6 small Meyer lemons or thin-skinned lemons (or Mexican limes, if you have them)	3 shallots, minced	¼ cup kosher salt
	3–4 garlic cloves, minced	¼ cup granulated sugar

In a pot of boiling water, blanch the lemons for about a minute. Drain, rinse, and wipe them with a paper towel to remove any wax.

Slice the lemons as thinly as you can, getting rid of any seeds and reserving the ends.

Combine the shallots and garlic together in one bowl. In another bowl, mix the salt and sugar. Place a layer of the lemon slices on the bottom of an airtight jar. Top this with a bit of the shallot-garlic mixture, then a good sprinkling of the salt-sugar mixture. Continue layering the lemon slices, alternating the two mixtures, until the jar is almost full but not overly packed. When you've filled the jar, press down gently on the layers to release some of their juices. Then, squeeze all the juice from the remaining lemon ends into the jar. Seal the jar tightly and shake a few times to circulate.

Refrigerate the jar for about 5 days, giving it a shake or two each day. Use the slices whole or chop roughly. They should keep, sealed in the refrigerator, for up to a month.

pickled red onions

RED ONIONS ARE A FAVORITE OF MINE BECAUSE THEY'RE SWEET, not to mention lovely to look at. You can certainly eat red onions raw, and they're remarkable when caramelized in olive oil due to their sugar content, but I think one of the best ways to treat a red onion is with a quick pickle. First, their natural sweetness combined with a bit more sugar ricochets off the vinegar, salt, and spice almost magically, creating a balance of flavor that tastes far more complex than you'd expect from so few and such simple ingredients. Second, the color of the onions seeps out into the liquid, so you'll find yourself with a jar of pink pickles swimming in a pool of preternaturally magenta brine. They're otherworldly and exactly the kind of condiment you want to have sitting on the table alongside a plate of sandwiches or bruschetta, a platter of tacos, or some spiced crab cakes. All that and these simple pickles take mere minutes to pull together. Assuming the entire jar isn't devoured immediately, they can also be stored in the fridge for up to 2 weeks, the flavor and color becoming more stunning as they macerate.

½ cup water

½ cup distilled white vinegar

3 tablespoons granulated sugar

1 teaspoon sea salt, plus more to taste

1 bay leaf, preferably fresh

1 dried red chile

1 red onion, thinly sliced into half-moons

In a small saucepan, combine the water, vinegar, sugar, salt, bay leaf, and chile and bring to a boil. Add the onion, reduce the heat, and simmer for 30 seconds. Remove from the heat and let cool completely. Transfer to an airtight jar and keep in the fridge for up to 2 weeks.

my marinated beans

IF I'M HONEST WITH MYSELF, I'M SOMEONE WHO MANAGES to be both high energy and lazy at the same time. (I know that sounds like a paradox.) But while one half of my DNA thrives in constant motion—*get that job*, *paint that room*, *move those hydrangea bushes*, *balance that checkbook*—the other half craves lying on the couch with a cat, a book, and a blanket—forever. Which is why I am, at least some of the time, an admittedly lazy home cook. Especially when it comes to beans. I know in my heart of hearts that I should always think ahead, soak the beans the night before, drain them, cook them, salt them, and then look lovingly at them, knowing I brought them from that dry and dormant state to a more tender and flavorful place with my own hands. But I rarely remember to do any of that and, frankly, I think canned beans are fine. Especially when you're going to dress them up with other flavorful ingredients and then let them marinate for a bit. So forgive yourself ahead of time if, like me, you choose to cheat a little here; life is way too short to beat yourself up over beans. *See an additional photograph on page 16.*

1 can (15.5 ounces) gigante beans, rinsed and drained, or 1 cup dried beans, cooked according to package directions

½ cup extra-virgin olive oil

Grated zest and juice of 1 lemon

2–3 garlic cloves, smashed

4–6 pepperoncini, trimmed and finely chopped

1–2 tablespoons fresh oregano leaves, roughly chopped

2–3 tablespoons sherry vinegar or other bright vinegar

Sea salt and freshly ground black pepper

Put the beans in a lidded mason jar large enough to hold the other ingredients as well. Add the olive oil, lemon zest and juice, garlic, pepperoncini, and oregano. Stir gently to combine so you don't smash the beans, and taste for brightness. Add enough sherry vinegar to give the marinade a bit of tang but not enough to overpower—the beans will get stronger as they sit.

Season the beans with salt and pepper and seal the jar. Let sit in the fridge for an hour or two, or overnight if possible. Give the jar a gentle shake every now and then to circulate the vinaigrette. Taste again and adjust the seasoning as needed. Serve straight from the jar with toothpicks for spearing (watch out for the smashed cloves of garlic, as they look remarkably like the beans after marinating).

smoked trout–stuffed deviled eggs

DEVILED EGGS ARE DECIDEDLY OLD-fashioned. They harken back to the days of crustless cucumber sandwiches and many-layered dips made from soup mixes. But it's kind of a shame, because I love hard-boiled eggs, and deviled eggs seem like they should be hard-boiled eggs on steroids. When I'm working, I regularly eat a hard-boiled egg and call it breakfast—or lunch. I'm only slightly embarrassed to admit that I recently could have been spotted walking down Sixth Avenue trying to elegantly peel a hard-boiled egg and sprinkle it with salt while running from one meeting to another. That's how much I love hard-boiled eggs. I'm just not a fan of adding gobs of mayonnaise to one of Mother Nature's most perfect foods. That said, over the years I've had to make many versions of deviled eggs for different cookbooks and magazine pieces I've styled, and have come to realize that the stuffy stuffed eggs I've long dismissed as dull are just one kind. There's another altogether delicious sort of devilishness out there, if you're open to it. Cut down on the mayonnaise, bid farewell to the ubiquitous paprika sprinkle, and this nostalgic little number we think of as dated can be refashioned into something cool and classic. With a hint of lemon, a spike of Dijon, and a bit of smoky trout swirled inside, suddenly the deviled egg is less frumpy and more fun; less Ethel and more Lucy. And really, who doesn't love Lucy?

8 large eggs	Juice of ½ lemon	Sea salt and freshly ground black pepper
¼ cup mayonnaise	2 ounces smoked trout, finely flaked	
1½ teaspoons Dijon mustard		Snipped fresh chives or chervil, for garnish

Bring a large pot of water to boil. Using a slotted spoon, gently lower the eggs into the boiling water, reduce to a simmer, cover, and let cook for 10 minutes. Set an alarm—seriously. When your alarm goes off, drain the eggs, run them under cold water, and set aside to cool.

Once the eggs are cool enough to handle, peel and halve them lengthwise. Remove the yolks and transfer them to a food processor. Set the whites aside.

Add the mayonnaise, mustard, lemon juice, and trout to the yolks and process until just smooth. Season with salt and pepper and transfer the mixture to a piping bag (you can always use a resealable plastic bag with the corner cut off for this bit).

Pipe the yolk mixture back into the whites, top with the herbs, and serve.

prosciutto, asparagus, and arugula rolls

GRAZING IS ALL ABOUT TASTING LOTS OF THINGS BUT not committing to a single one. It's the opposite of meal monogamy, the antithesis of boredom at the table. When you graze, you skip from dish to dish, bending the rules of convention like a culinary contortionist. Instead of saying, "Tonight I'll have a salad," you flirt first with that dish of briny Cerignola olives to your left, mingle shamelessly with that come-hither-looking bowl of artichokes on your right, and make an absolute spectacle of yourself with the wild mushroom crostini across the way. You scan the table looking for your next conquest, and then you set your sights on barely blanched asparagus spears and baby arugula, dressed with olive oil and lemon and rolled up in velum-thin layers of prosciutto. An Italian-inspired twist on negimaki, these are one of my most reliable kitchen tricks—equal parts easy, impressive, and irresistible. *See an additional photograph on page 17.*

Sea salt	Grated zest and juice of 1 lemon	2–3 handfuls baby or wild arugula
1 pound pencil-thin asparagus, trimmed	Freshly ground black pepper	16 thin slices prosciutto (about ½ pound), each about 8" long
3 tablespoons extra-virgin olive oil		

Bring a large pot of salted water to boil. Add the asparagus to the pot and cook until bright green and just tender, about 3 minutes depending on thickness. Drain the asparagus and run immediately under cold water to stop the cooking process. Pat dry and set aside.

In a large bowl, whisk together the olive oil, lemon zest, and about half the lemon juice. Season with salt and pepper. Add the arugula and asparagus spears to the bowl and toss gently to coat, being careful not to snap the asparagus. Taste and add a bit more lemon juice if necessary.

On a large cutting board or work surface, arrange 4 slices of prosciutto vertically and slightly overlapping to form a 6" × 8" rectangle. Lay one-quarter of the dressed arugula and asparagus horizontally across the prosciutto on the end closest to you. Tightly roll up the prosciutto as you would a jelly roll, being sure to keep the vegetables evenly distributed.

Cut the rolls on the bias into 8 pieces and repeat with the remaining ingredients.

homemade croutons with parmesan shavings on baby romaine
(aka deconstructed caesar salad)

THE SAME THING ALWAYS HAPPENS WHEN I MAKE Caesar salad: I set the big wooden bowl full of salad down on the table and go back into the kitchen to finish whatever else I'm cooking. When I return, all evidence of the essential croutons and Parmesan shavings have vanished. A bowl of gently dressed lettuce, devoid of all garnishes, stares at me. How, you may wonder, do so many crunchy croutons just disappear? How does a pile of paper-thin cheese just evaporate? Well, it's The Ken Effect. In a blatant expression of grazing, Ken has made a habit of ransacking my Caesar salad for what he calls "the good bits" before dinner even begins. This pattern became so pervasive that I finally decided to legitimize the whole sneaky affair. So here it is—croutons and cheese served in leaves of baby romaine and dressed with a brazen garlicky-anchovy dressing. It's incidental grazing food at its best.

3–4 cups cubed rustic bread

2 tablespoons plus ¼ cup extra-virgin olive oil

Salt and freshly ground black pepper

A couple sprigs fresh oregano or thyme, leaves picked

1–2 anchovy fillets, or to taste

2–3 tablespoons fresh lemon juice

1 garlic clove, smashed

1 head baby romaine lettuce, leaves separated

Fresh Parmesan shavings

Preheat the oven to 400°F.

Place the bread cubes on a rimmed baking sheet and drizzle with 2 tablespoons of olive oil. Sprinkle with salt, pepper, and herbs and toss to coat well. Bake for 8 to 12 minutes, turning the cubes at least once so they brown evenly on all sides. Remove from the oven and set aside to cool.

Place the anchovies on a cutting board and chop them, then use the side of your knife to mash them into a paste. Transfer the anchovies to a small, lidded jar and add the remaining ¼ cup olive oil, the lemon juice, and garlic clove. Season with salt and pepper and seal the jar before shaking well. Set aside.

Place the individual romaine leaves on a platter. Fill each leaf with a few croutons and top with a shaving or two of Parmesan. Drizzle the dressing over the entire platter, sprinkle with pepper, and serve.

communal salade niçoise

I HAVE LOVED *SALADE NIÇOISE* **FOR AS LONG AS I CAN** remember. I once ate one in a small seaside town on the southern coast of France under a colorfully striped awning; I enjoyed one with my friend Jackie and her newborn son on Rue Cler in Paris; I've had a smattering of good and not-so-good versions in and around New York over the years. But the majority of my best Niçoise-eating experiences happened courtesy of Pastis, an oh-so-fashionable spot, sadly now shuttered, in the Meatpacking District in NYC near our apartment. For us, Pastis was reliably good French food close to home, but it was also the kind of place that could claim a crowd nearly all the time, to the point where on more than one occasion, we'd walk over only to be told it would take an hour or more to be seated. Rather than being deterred, we learned to adapt. We would leave the hostess with her lengthy list of names, head home, order takeout, and enjoy the same lovely meal in the comfort of our apartment in less than 30 minutes. Creatures of habit that we are, we nearly always ordered the same thing: a medium cheeseburger with fries and a Niçoise salad. Ken was partial to the burger and I was devoted to the fresh, barely seared tuna Niçoise, but we always shared. The salad was perfect for splitting because there was more than enough for two. My version is less traditional—I've swapped fresh tuna for the meaty pink Italian kind that comes packed in olive oil; I'm partial to substituting roasted tomatoes if fresh aren't truly in season; and I suggest creamy green olives instead of the traditional black—but the communal concept is the same. Everyone gets a little bit of everything with only one plate to wash.

recipe continues

communal salade niçoise

8 small new potatoes, halved

Sea salt

Good handful haricots verts, trimmed

2–3 anchovy fillets, or to taste

1 garlic clove, smashed

¼ cup extra-virgin olive oil

Grated zest and juice of 1 lemon

Freshly ground black pepper

2 small heads gem butter lettuce

1 jar or can (5–7 ounces) Italian tuna in olive oil, drained

4 large hard-boiled eggs

8–10 cherry tomatoes, fresh or oven-roasted (page 64)

1 cup Cerignola olives or other buttery olives

Put the potatoes in a pot of salted water and bring to a boil over high heat. When the water boils, reduce the heat to medium and simmer until the potatoes are just tender and can be pierced with a knife, about 8 minutes. Use a slotted spoon to transfer the potatoes to a bowl to cool.

Return the water to a boil, add the haricots verts, and cook until the water returns to a boil and the beans are just bright green and crisp-tender, 1 to 2 minutes. Drain and run under cold water to stop the cooking process.

Meanwhile, put the anchovies and garlic on a cutting board and chop them together. Then use the side of your knife to mash them even more, until nearly a paste. Transfer the mixture to a small lidded jar and add the olive oil and lemon zest and juice. Season with salt and pepper, seal the jar, and shake well.

Separate the leaves of lettuce and lay them on a platter or board. Scatter the potatoes over the lettuce and spoon the tuna evenly around the platter. Halve the eggs and spread them around evenly as well, then add the tomatoes, haricots verts, and olives. To serve, drizzle some of the dressing over the platter and serve the rest alongside.

melon soup with prosciutto shards

A SLICE OF CANTALOUPE OR HONEYDEW MELON swathed in a sheet of prosciutto—when the melon is so ripe that the juices seep to the skin as soon as it's pierced with a knife, and the ham has that fatty, nutty, almost feral mountain flavor to it, you know within an instant why this is such classic Italian fare. The balance of sweet and salty is at the heart of it, and this summer soup captures just that. With crisped pieces of prosciutto scattered over the chilled, liquid melon, it's both familiar and surprising. On a hot summer afternoon, when I want nothing more than to sit on the patio with a thick book, watch the hawk circle silently up in the sky, and be entertained by the chipmunks darting amongst the rocks and ferns, this is the lunch I crave: a cup of this soup alongside a sandwich of Ham and Cornichons on Buttered Baguette (page 45).

6–8 slices prosciutto, halved lengthwise

1 small honeydew or cantaloupe melon, halved, seeded, and cut into chunks

¼ cup fresh lime juice

1 tablespoon honey (optional)

Sea salt and freshly ground black pepper

Preheat the oven to 400°F. Line a baking sheet with parchment paper or foil.

Lay the prosciutto slices on the lined baking sheet and toast until just crisp, about 8 minutes. Remove and set aside to cool.

Meanwhile, put the melon chunks in a blender and puree until very smooth. Add the lime juice and honey (if using), season with salt and pepper, and puree again. Taste, adjust the seasoning as needed, and chill slightly. Serve the soup in small bowls or shot glasses topped with a shard of prosciutto.

avocado, as it should be

THIS IS NOT A RECIPE. IT'S JUST A PERFECT THING IN A very imperfect world. And it has to be here—to overlook it in a book about fast, easy ways to eat good food would be heresy. Growing up in California, we had three avocado trees in our front yard, and while the squirrels usually got away with a fair number of them—we would find the half-eaten fruit and random pits on the patio all the time— we were still well-endowed with bags of the creamy, coal-skinned gems throughout the year. We often ate them either right out of the skin with a spoon or barely smashed in a bowl—near naked and far from smooth. Which is probably the reason why the addition of onion, garlic, tomatoes, chiles, or almost anything else to a mashed avocado makes me cringe. A good avocado needs no competition in the bowl, just a squeeze of citrus and a sprinkle of salt. This is my mayonnaise, the spread that makes any sandwich better, a slice of toast a complete meal, and bag of chips almost irrelevant. Put this out with An Unconventional Plate of Vegetables (page 2) and a good loaf of bread, and you're set. *See photograph on next page.*

2 Hass avocados	1 lime	Sea salt

Halve the avocados and remove the pits. Scoop the flesh into a bowl and mash with a fork until chunky but spreadable. Season with lime juice and sea salt, to taste. Devour with a spoon or serve with tortilla chips, fresh vegetables, or toast.

FOLLOWING PAGE: *Avocado, As It Should Be* | *Tuna Crudo with Tomatillo-Avocado Dressing* (PAGE 58) | *Crab, Avocado, and Black Bean Tostadas* (PAGE 59)

lemony hummus

THERE WILL BE CONTROVERSY HERE. I WILL FACE dissenters. I realize it's a subject that engenders deep and passionate feelings, but here goes: When it comes to my hummus, I can take or leave the tahini. I know, some will say it isn't actually hummus without the tahini, but from my quick research on the matter, *hummus* translates from Arabic as "chickpeas." Enough said. Well, almost: The addition of tahini, known as *hummus bi tahina*, wasn't noted until the 13th century in Cairo. But I'm not trying to be difficult. The fact is, I love chickpeas mashed up with a little garlic and cumin and a lot of lemon and olive oil. (Okay, worth noting: Lemon and garlic weren't added to hummus until even later than tahini, according to my online research. But why get hung up on details?) To my taste, if you've got chickpeas, olive oil, lemon, garlic, and cumin, you can stop right there. Everything that happened to me earlier in the day—the guy who shoved past me on the subway; the taxi that sped by and splattered filthy water on my jeans; right now, my upstairs neighbor who is wearing stilettos and dancing to ABBA while I try to write—all of that will be forgotten with a generous spoonful of hummus, regardless of the tahini. But I'm okay with adding it, too—I just don't think it's any less hummus if you don't have tahini in the house. *See photograph on page 40.*

1 can (15.5 ounces) chickpeas, rinsed and drained	¼–½ cup extra-virgin olive oil, plus more as needed	1–2 teaspoons ground cumin, or to taste
1 garlic clove, peeled		Sea salt and freshly ground black pepper
2 tablespoons tahini (optional)	2–3 tablespoons fresh lemon juice, or to taste	

In a food processor, combine the chickpeas, garlic, and tahini (if using) and blitz until the mixture is coarsely chopped. With the machine running, begin to add the olive oil through the feed tube in a steady stream, starting with ¼ cup. Continue to process until the mixture begins to look smooth, adding more oil until you have a creamy puree.

Add a couple tablespoons of lemon juice, 1 teaspoon cumin, and some salt and pepper and pulse again. At this point, taste the mixture and adjust the flavor as needed for your palate. I prefer more lemon and cumin than tahini in my hummus, but some people love that rich, nutty flavor and want more tahini—make it yours.

rosemary and white bean smear

THERE ARE TWO SPECIFIC "DIPS" I REMEMBER MY mom serving for guests when I was a kid. The first was a caviar cream cheese that she'd buy at the Farmers Market in Hollywood at Monsieur Marcel. Not the modern-day farmers' market, but the original market that first opened back in 1934 on Fairfax and West 3rd Street. A wonder of covered kiosks hawking all kinds of specialty foods, the market was full of small family-run shops selling everything from homemade ice cream to seafood, and of course, the famed Du-par's Pie Shop. When we lived in Laurel Canyon, this was the place my mom would frequent to procure bits and pieces for entertaining—and the legendary pink caviar dip was always among them. It was the Katharine Hepburn of appetizers: classic and sublimely sophisticated, the patrician of predinner spreads. The other dip she served was a white bean puree she'd make herself. A rustic blend of cannellini beans, rosemary, lemon zest, lemon juice, and olive oil, this dip was less fancy and more earthy, less glamorous and more quirky. A few years ago, I was home in LA and my parents and I went to the original Farmers Market, found the caviar cheese, and bought a small container to see if it lived up to expectations from 30-plus years ago. It's remarkable how flavors live on in your mind; it was just as we'd all remembered. But I can't lie: As much as I love Hepburn, I'm still partial to this less Hollywood, more homey approach. *See photograph on page 40.*

1 can (15.5 ounces) cannellini beans, rinsed and drained	1 tablespoon chopped fresh rosemary, plus more as needed	Grated zest of 1 lemon
1 garlic clove, peeled	¼–½ cup extra-virgin olive oil, plus more as needed	1 tablespoon fresh lemon juice, or to taste
		Sea salt and freshly ground black pepper

In a food processor, combine the beans, garlic, and rosemary and puree until the mixture is coarsely chopped. With the machine running, begin to add the olive oil through the feed tube in a steady stream, starting with ¼ cup. Continue to process until the mixture begins to look smooth, adding more oil until you have a creamy puree.

Add the lemon zest and juice, sprinkle with salt and pepper, and pulse again. Taste the puree and add more rosemary, lemon juice, or salt and pepper as needed.

parmesan pea spread

I LOVE FRESH PEAS. I EVEN LOVE SHELLING PEAS: THE WAY THE pods pop when they're just off the vine; how the peas lie in their emerald cocoon lined up from barely-there to brazenly plump; how my fingers smell fertile and mossy after all the shells have been emptied of their virescent pearls. Fresh peas are a treat, a seasonal romance I look forward to all winter that's far too fleeting, which is why my freezer is rarely without a box of the frozen kind. Captured at their peak, frozen peas are reliable in flavor and dependable when you have nothing fresh in the house.

Derived many moons ago from a risotto recipe by Nigella Lawson, I've turned this commonsense combo of peas, butter, and Parmesan into a spread for crostini, smeared it on a pizza crust for something unexpected, loosened it with cream and served it over pasta, and even thinned it with chicken stock for a refreshing summer soup (page 87). Like with many recipes in my repertoire, I use the basic idea for many different dishes; but in its purest form, I smear it on toast.

½ stick (4 tablespoons) unsalted butter, at room temperature

1 tablespoon minced shallot (about ½ shallot)

3 cups fresh peas or 1 box (10 ounces) frozen peas

½ cup chicken stock

½ cup freshly grated Parmesan cheese, or more to taste

Salt and freshly ground black pepper

Fresh mint leaves, for garnish

In a large saucepan, melt 2 tablespoons of the butter over medium heat. Add the shallot and cook until just soft, 3 to 4 minutes. Add the peas and swirl them around in the butter until nicely coated, then increase the heat to medium-high and add the chicken stock. Bring the stock to a simmer and cook the peas until they're tender but still bright green, no more than 2 or 3 minutes for frozen peas or about 5 minutes for fresh.

Carefully transfer the pea mixture to a food processor and add the remaining 2 tablespoons butter and the Parmesan. Puree the mixture until smooth. Season with salt and pepper and adjust the seasoning as needed (add more cheese, if you like).

I serve this spread on toasted bread with a mint leaf and another good shave of cheese, but if you like the idea of adding mint to the puree, feel free to add a few leaves to the mix; just be cautious—the mint can overpower the delicate sweetness of the peas if you have a heavy hand.

CLOCKWISE, FROM TOP: *Japanese Eggplant Mousse with Za'atar* (PAGE 42) | *Lemony Hummus* (PAGE 38) | *Parmesan Pea Spread* | *Rosemary and White Bean Smear* (PAGE 39)

japanese eggplant mousse with za'atar

I REMEMBER THE FIRST TIME I MET MARK Bittman (the man who gets a large chunk of credit for my having the pinch-worthy job that I do). It was, for all intents and purposes, a job interview, and I had the requisite butterflies one gets—maybe more, as this was someone I held in high esteem. Dressed in a well-worn sweater and sneakers, Mark was sitting amongst stacks of cookbooks and papers, down one of the alleys of desks that made up the hustle and bustle of the *New York Times* newsroom floor, right in the midst of the ringing phones and clattering keys. Within minutes, despite his culinary gravitas, my nerves were assuaged by his casual manner; he was a bastion of calm in contrast to the constant blur and hum of people moving and talking and writing all around us. We sat at his desk and talked for a little over an hour, until he only slightly abruptly turned to me, stood up, and said with a distinct sense of finality, "Okay, I have to go home and eat an eggplant." And with that, I was dismissed. A few minutes later, as I was walking down 42nd Street, I ran through our meeting in my head, trying to recall what I'd said or how I'd come off, but I couldn't focus. I simply kept hearing how firmly yet charmingly he'd bid me farewell, an au revoir laced with information: his intent to leave and eat an eggplant. All I could do was wonder how he'd prepare that eggplant, patiently waiting for his return home. *See photograph on page 40.*

3 medium Japanese eggplant or baby eggplant, halved lengthwise

¼–½ cup extra-virgin olive oil

Sea salt

2 garlic cloves, unpeeled

Grated zest of 1 lemon

1–2 teaspoons fresh lemon juice, or to taste

3–4 teaspoons za'atar

¼ cup finely chopped fresh Italian parsley

Preheat the oven to 400°F.

Brush the cut sides of each eggplant half with olive oil and sprinkle with salt. Place the eggplant halves cut-side up on a baking sheet along with the garlic. Roast until the flesh of the eggplant is extremely tender and can be easily scooped with a spoon, about 30 minutes.

Scoop the eggplant flesh into a food processor. Squeeze the garlic out of its skins and add to the eggplant. Add the lemon zest and juice. With the machine running, add ¼ cup of the olive oil through the feed tube in a steady stream. Continue to process until the mixture is light and fluffy, like a mousse. Transfer to a bowl and gently fold in the za'atar and parsley. Taste and season with more salt, lemon juice, or za'atar as needed.

pan con tomate

WHEN YOU LOOK AT *PAN CON TOMATE*, IT DOESN'T SEEM like much. In fact, it can look sort of sad, a slice of toast smeared with a translucent red spread, nothing as luscious as jam and, if done properly, barely there in thickness; a hushed little snack, utterly undecorated, like a cake not yet frosted. But then, you taste it. The startling pungency of the anchovies is quickly softened by the sweet but acidic tomato, all followed up with a throaty whisper of garlic. Quiet only in appearances, a proper *pan con tomate* is like walking into a grand old house with faded walls and declining splendor, furniture covered in bed linens like ghosts, and pale light streaming through sagging windows. But then you pull off the sheets to reveal the thick velvet and button-studded couches in all shades of claret and sapphire, see the marbled-topped tables and mahogany-footed chairs, take in the crystal chandelier, and open the windows to a sudden burst of sea-laced air that floods the room. A good *pan con tomate* is just like that: shrouded in quiet and low expectations until the first bite, when it transforms into a wonder of flavor and complexity. Grating the tomatoes matters, smashing the anchovies well is essential, and while you traditionally swipe the toast with raw garlic, if you—or someone you know (my husband, for instance)—find raw garlic a bit too bold, you can use roasted garlic to fabulous effect. It's sweeter and creamier but adds a welcome earthiness in place of the fiery bite. *See photograph on page xiii.*

2 large tomatoes	Sea salt and freshly ground black pepper	2 or so large garlic cloves, peeled
3–4 good-quality anchovy fillets	12 slices (½" each) country bread	

Set a box grater inside a bowl large enough to hold it and grate the tomatoes using the side with the largest holes—you should end up with a slightly thick, juicy, pulpy mixture. Grate as much of each tomato as possible, until all that's left are the remnants of some skin; discard this.

Add the anchovies to the grated tomato and, using a fork, mash them until they're relatively well blended. Taste the mixture and decide if you need to add some salt— the anchovies are pretty salty, so you may not. Sprinkle with a bit of pepper.

Preheat the broiler. Place the bread slices on a baking sheet and toast until they just begin to brown. Remove from the oven and rub the top of each slice of toast with a clove of garlic until lightly coated.

Using a butter knife, top each piece of toast with a thin smear of the tomato mixture and serve.

ham and cornichons on buttered baguette

KEN WILL BE THE FIRST TO TELL YOU THAT I have some serious food quirks. For one, I hate when he buys a muffin or scone or some other breakfast product at a chain coffee bar. I know what they'll taste like (not much beyond sweet), I know there's nothing good in them, and I know that if he'd just wait a little while (till we get home), he'd enjoy something so much better. Sometimes I actually think he buys that lemon–poppy seed lump of starch and sugar just to bug me. But what can I do?

Then there's my airplane food issue. I won't eat airplane food. Ever. You could put me on a flight to Australia, tell me there's a 9-hour delay on the tarmac, and I still wouldn't give in. Happily, this scenario never arises because I am notorious for packing an airplane picnic. The day before a trip, when I'm running around doing laundry, cleaning the house, and making sure there's sufficient cat food on hand, I always allow an hour or so to shop for our mile-high meal—and it's almost always the same thing. My fear of flying keeps me consistent, like a baseball player who always wears his winning pair of socks. The idea that I had this exact meal on our last flight and made it safely back to earth gives me a sense of security. Thinly sliced French-style ham with tangy cornichons and lots of salty butter on a baguette is my talisman; it's the perfect food at 35,000 feet. It may actually be the perfect sandwich period. (Author's note: In case you ever happen to sit next to me, you should know that we do detour from eating this sandwich once a year, on the flight home from LA after Thanksgiving. On that trip, we always have leftover turkey and avocado on sourdough. Again, all in the name of safety.)

1 baguette, about 18"	8–12 thin slices jambon de Paris or other French-style cooked ham	14–16 cornichons, halved
Salted butter (preferably a European-style butter, such as Chimay or Kerrygold)		Toothpicks, as needed

Slice the baguette lengthwise and generously smear both sides with salty butter (you really can't over-butter this sandwich, in my opinion). Drape the ham slices in gentle folds over the bottom half of the loaf and then top with the cornichon halves.

Place the nicely buttered top half over the bottom of the loaf and secure the sandwich with toothpicks at 8 to 12 even intervals. Use a bread knife to cut the sandwich evenly into slices between the toothpicks and serve. If, by chance, you're not serving this to guests but packing it for a flight instead, cut it for only as many as you're planning to share with (I suggest no more than one), wrap tightly in foil, and pack in your carry-on along with a bag of salted potato chips.

sardine bruschetta with fennel and preserved lemons

WHEN I USE TINNED SARDINES, WHICH IS admittedly a lot, I keep it simple. They're so vibrant on their own that you don't really want to do anything that will compete with their tender, briny meatiness. Fennel and lemon are two flavors that, while potent in their own right, do work really well with sardines, not by overpowering them but by gently softening out their bolder edges. The sweet licorice of the fennel mellows the fish, and the salty-sweet preserved lemons brighten the buttery flavor. Of course, you can take the easy approach and add some fresh lemon zest and juice into the mix if you don't have preserved lemons around, but there is something more robust about the garlic-shallot-sugar-salt-sour mix that brings it all to life.

1 bulb fennel, halved and cored (fronds reserved)	1 cup Preserved Lemons (page 22), with some of the juices	2 cans (3.75 ounces each) oil-packed sardines
	Sea salt and freshly ground black pepper	12 slices rustic bread, toasted

Use a mandoline to cut the fennel halves into paper-thin slices and then transfer to a medium bowl.

Roughly chop the preserved lemons until they resemble a relish and add them to the fennel along with any juices—the idea is to let the liquid from the lemons dress the raw fennel and then allow it all to macerate. Season with salt and pepper as needed.

While the fennel and lemons sit, drain the sardines of their oil and place them in a small bowl. Use a fork to mash the sardines into a rough paste. If the mixture seems a bit dry, add a teaspoon or so of the oil from the can. You want the paste to be spreadable, but you don't want it to lose all texture.

To serve, spread about a teaspoon of the sardine paste on each slice of toast and add a tangle of the fennel-lemon mixture. Top each toast with a pinch of fresh fennel fronds.

creamy avocado soup with crab

BAJA CALIFORNIA, JUST OVER THE BORDER FROM SAN Diego, is a place we'd sometimes go to shop on a Saturday when I was young. Tijuana was where we went most often, but my parents had a friend named Lil with a house on Rosarita Beach, and one day we went down just to visit her for lunch. Lil always struck me as *almost* glamorous—she was older than my parents, probably 50, single, and a successful realtor in west Los Angeles. She had the white-gold hair that women of a certain age possess, wore pastel-colored slacks (yes, slacks) with color-coordinated blouses, and her skin was gently lined and papery, swept over with powder and a bit of blush. She wasn't an aging movie star, but she had a manicured quality and carried herself like someone comfortable moving through life alone. I recall this trip more specifically than others because of the lunch she made. Sitting at her rattan table with matching cushioned chairs overlooking the expanse of sand and far-off blue, I watched as Lil brought out a platter of avocado halves, each filled with shrimp or crab in the vacancy where the slippery pit had been. At the age of 8 or so, using the fruit itself as an edible bowl struck me as pure brilliance—not only did I get to eat the shellfish salad she stuffed into the center, but then I was left with an entire avocado half and a spoon. The combination was magical. This soup is a riff on that combination; it's more dressed up than Lil's simple lunch, but the flavors are spot-on.

2 avocados, cut into chunks	¼ teaspoon cayenne pepper, or more to taste	1 teaspoon finely minced jalapeño
1 cup buttermilk	Sea salt and freshly ground black pepper	2–3 sprigs fresh cilantro, leaves chopped
2 tablespoons fresh lime juice	½ pound lump crabmeat, picked over for shells	Extra-virgin olive oil, for serving

In a food processor or blender, combine the avocados and buttermilk and puree until very smooth. Add 1 tablespoon of the lime juice and the cayenne, season with salt and pepper, and blend again. Adjust the seasoning as needed.

In a small bowl, combine the crab with the jalapeño, cilantro, and the remaining 1 tablespoon lime juice. Season with salt and pepper.

Spoon the soup into small bowls, top with a scoop of the crab mixture, and drizzle with olive oil.

three-tomato panzanella

I HAVE A THEORY ABOUT RESTAURANTS. I BELIEVE THAT HOW good a restaurant is can be judged by how good (or not good) their bread is. Sit down at a restaurant and find yourself face-to-face with a thick slice of toothsome, slightly sour peasant bread—the crumb freckled with wheat and full of holes, the crust blistered with char and strewn with flour—and you're probably about to eat well. Reach into the napkin-lined basket and emerge with a hunk of snow-white sponge, the skin soft and pallid, perhaps even a bit moist, and you should probably go elsewhere. Good bread can also make a just-okay meal seem better: "Well, at least the bread is really good." It can be the highlight of a meal or a deal-breaker.

With this recipe, an interpretation of the traditional Italian bread salad, the bread is a deal-breaker. Great bread will make this, but the inverse is also true: Bad bread, or even mediocre, will break your heart. The bread needs to be dry so that it can soak up all the juices of the salad and still hold its spring; if the bread is too soft or fresh, it will turn mushy. What you want is bread with some tug to it, lots of nice crevices in the crumb, and a sturdy crust. When the cubes macerate in the salad, they become sodden and animated with flavor, unresisting and softened to the chew. We make this as an excuse to use up all the heels of bread that build up in our house; when the tomatoes are at their peak and the herbs are resplendent, it's the perfect expression of summer.

recipe continues

three-tomato panzanella

1 loaf day-old good-quality rustic bread

1 pint red cherry tomatoes, halved

1 pint yellow cherry tomatoes, halved

2–3 medium Green Zebra tomatoes, cut into wedges

Sea salt and freshly ground black pepper

½ red onion, cut into thin half-moons

2 tablespoons small capers, drained

1 celery heart, finely sliced (leaves reserved)

¼ cup extra-virgin olive oil, plus more as needed

2–3 tablespoons red wine vinegar

6–8 anchovy fillets, very finely chopped

1 garlic clove, peeled

3–4 sprigs fresh basil, leaves picked

Make sure your bread is truly stale—if not, cut the bread into thick slices and then tear into big pieces (about 1"). Let them sit out in the air for an hour or more, or toast for a couple of minutes, not for color but just to dry them out.

In a large bowl, combine the tomatoes with a sprinkle of salt and pepper and let sit for a few minutes (the salt will help draw some of the juices out of the tomatoes). Then add the red onion, capers, celery, and bread and toss well to combine.

In a small bowl or jar, combine the olive oil, vinegar, and anchovies. Grate the garlic into the mix with a rasp-style zester/grater. Whisk or shake well. Drizzle the dressing over the salad, toss, adjust the seasoning as needed, and then add the basil leaves and celery leaves. Let the salad sit for 15 minutes or longer to macerate and then serve.

persian cucumbers, snap peas, and red onion with lemon zest

KEN AND I HAVE A SUBTLE YET ONGOING difference of opinion when it comes to peeling vegetables. I don't think a tender young carrot needs more than a good scrub, but he adamantly disagrees. I prefer to leave the skin on my eggplant, and he finds it tough (we meet in the middle on this one, and I peel the ink-toned vegetables in alternating strips so we each get a bit of what we like). This clash of culinary tastes is why Persian (mini) cucumbers are such a welcome vegetable in our house—they're a natural compromise, the perfect peacekeeper. With tender barely-there skins, you don't need to peel them, and they have a more lush and fertile flavor than their larger, thicker-skinned cousins. Paired with sweet, crisp snap peas, slivers of red onion, and a tangy vinaigrette, these slinky cucumbers are like the United Nations of vegetables, bringing everyone together for a summer salad of delicious proportions. *See photograph on page* 77.

3 tablespoons extra-virgin olive oil

Grated zest and juice of 1 lemon

1 tablespoon country-style Dijon mustard

Sea salt and freshly ground black pepper

3 Persian (mini) cucumbers, sliced into ribbons

2 cups sugar snap peas, cut on the bias

½ red onion, thinly sliced into half-moons

¼–½ cup crumbled goat or feta cheese (optional)

In a small jar or bowl, combine the olive oil, lemon zest and juice, and mustard and season with salt and pepper. Shake or whisk well to emulsify.

In a large bowl, combine the cucumbers, snap peas, and onion. Drizzle with enough of the dressing to just coat the vegetables. Add the cheese (if using) and serve.

peak of summer salad

I GREW UP IN CALIFORNIA. HAVING LIVED now for many years on the East Coast, I have adapted pretty well to the differences between the two, but there are still things I miss. Even though my friends and family back home begin to fret about forest fires at the first bluster, I can't help but long for the ghostly Santa Ana winds that blow through Los Angeles each year; those enveloping hot gusts that Joan Didion described as ". . . the season of suicide and divorce and prickly dread;" those menacing gales that Raymond Chandler noted were when "meek little wives feel the edge of the carving knife and study their husbands' necks. Anything can happen." Like Halloween, for me those powerful breezes are spooky and seductive at the same time, an expression of my native home. I still crave watching the sun set from the bluffs above Pacific Coast Highway. I ache for the smell of eucalyptus and wild fennel that blankets the bone-dry hills, and I'll never stop yearning to live in a place where avocados and oranges grow on trees in every yard you pass, or to be surrounded by walls of bougainvillea hugging the sides of houses, their flowers thin as tissue paper in every color of pink and orange.

But one thing that I have come to love about living in a place with seasons is the longing it creates, the desire for one period of time to end and the next to begin. After a tediously long winter, the arrival of warmth is so welcome that you breathe a sigh of relief; it's like an old friend getting back in touch after being away for far too long, someone you worried might have forgotten they promised to return, but then suddenly reappears as though never having gone. It's the softening in the shoulders you feel on that first day when you can leave the jacket behind, the tanning of cheeks after a day in the sun, and the taste of peaches, tomatoes, and corn after months without. Living on the East Coast is a constant lesson in patience, a practice in fortitude, but one that's rewarded so sweetly that it's very hard to leave.

2 large heirloom tomatoes, chopped	½ red onion, halved and thinly sliced	Juice of 1 lemon
3 large peaches, chopped	A few sprigs fresh cilantro, leaves picked	Sea salt and freshly ground black pepper
2 ears corn, kernels removed from the cobs	¼ cup extra-virgin olive oil	

In a large bowl, combine the tomatoes, peaches, corn, red onion, and cilantro and toss gently. In a jar or small bowl, combine the olive oil and lemon juice and season with salt and pepper. Taste and adjust the seasoning as needed. Drizzle the salad with the dressing and toss.

zucchini ribbons with herbed goat cheese
(grilled or raw)

ONCE SUMMER ROLLS AROUND, KEN AND I eat an absurd amount of zucchini. Come early June, I head to our local farm stand each Friday, a sloping lean-to on Route 7 where tables barely off the road stand burdened with summer's bounty, and I lose all sense of self-control. Along with downy-skinned peaches, milky corn, and tomatoes in every shade from honey to oxblood, there are also masses of zucchini, and I just can't resist. Their delicate skin is burnished a rich magnolia green and their lithe figures go slightly swollen at the base. I'd like to say we prepare these squash differently each time, slicing them for a gratin, grating them for a bread, sautéing them for a soup, or roasting them, stuffed with herbs and cheese, but we don't. Pretty much all we ever seem to garner the energy or ingenuity to do with them is this: We thinly slice them with a vegetable peeler or mandoline until they resemble ribbons, toss them with lemon juice, olive oil, and a bit of salt and pepper, spear them with skewers, bending each back and forth on top of themselves like a switchback road, and let them char on the grill. When we're really lazy, we eat them raw—tender and wilted in nothing more than the bracing vinaigrette. *See photograph on page 109.*

1 small log goat cheese, at room temperature	3–4 sprigs fresh tarragon, chervil, or dill, leaves picked and torn	4 medium zucchini, trimmed
4 tablespoons extra-virgin olive oil, plus more as needed	Grated zest and juice of 1 lemon	½ red onion, cut into very thin half-moons (optional)
	Sea salt and freshly ground black pepper	

Put the goat cheese in a small bowl along with 1 tablespoon of the olive oil. Use a spatula or wooden spoon to cream the cheese until almost spreadable, adding a bit more oil if needed. Add the herbs and mix thoroughly to combine. Let sit.

In a large bowl, combine the remaining 3 tablespoons olive oil with the lemon zest and juice. Season with salt and pepper and whisk to combine. Use a mandoline or vegetable peeler to slice the zucchini lengthwise into long, very thin ribbons, adding them to the bowl with the dressing to marinate and soften.

Preheat a grill. Skewer the squash, folding each ribbon back and forth two or three times. Lightly grill the skewers over medium heat until the squash is tender.

Serve the reserved goat cheese crumbled over the top of either the grilled or simply marinated raw zucchini.

scallop and plum ceviche with tarragon

IN CULINARY SCHOOL, WE HAD WHAT were called "Market Basket" exams. On those days, we were paired up with another student and then given a few key ingredients (the Market Basket) and told to create a three-course meal in a set amount of time—a meal that the chef instructor would then taste and grade based on originality, flavor, and presentation. In addition to the Market Basket ingredients, we were allowed to use pantry basics to accentuate the recipes we created, but the core ingredients we were assigned had to be the focus of the menu. For my favorite Market Basket exam, I was paired with my closest friend in the class, Kevin. We had a very similar approach to food and cooking, and we had fun together in the kitchen, so as far as tests go, that one was more enjoyable than stressful. That day, two of the ingredients we were given were scallops and plums—not a pairing I would naturally make on my own, but that's the point. Together, Kevin and I concocted a less-than-traditional ceviche that we flavored with fresh, licorice-y tarragon and lip-puckering lime juice. Like with most ceviche, the fish cooks in the acid of the citrus, infusing the scallops with a brightness that's refreshing but doesn't overpower the sweetness of the meat or the flesh of the fruit. It's a delicate dish; a virtue further enhanced as the juice of the plums seeps into the scallops, giving everything a gentle and otherworldly lavender hue. As I recall, we also made a chilled asparagus soup that day. Using both green and white asparagus, we made two separate batches—one vibrant green and the other creamy white—and then swirled them together in the bowl. There was also a savory crostata involved. In retrospect, the entire Market Basket menu we created was an exercise in how to cook for those of us who love to graze. Use what you've got to make lots of good little things, including this ceviche.

1 pound sea scallops, cut into ¼"–½" dice

2 black plums, cut into ¼"–½" dice

1–2 sprigs fresh tarragon, leaves picked and chopped, or more to taste

½ teaspoon grated lime zest

¼ cup fresh lime juice

Pinch cayenne pepper

Sea salt

In a bowl, toss together the scallops, plums, tarragon, lime zest and juice, and cayenne. Season with salt. Chill the mixture for about 15 minutes. Taste and adjust the seasoning.

tuna crudo with tomatillo-avocado dressing

THIS IS ALL ABOUT THE DRESSING. FRESH, flavorful sushi-grade tuna is heavenly, and it's also the perfect partner for this zesty drizzle; but if you don't eat tuna or don't partake of raw fish, don't turn the page. This dressing is what I make to slather over tacos, tamales, or almost any Mexican-inspired dish that needs a little oomph, from simple Saturday quesadilla lunches to lazy weeknight salads when I have nothing more than some fresh corn, tomatoes, and a can of black beans in the house. It's the salsa-cum-dressing that just makes everything better. Tossed with crab for a spunky salad, spread on grilled corn, or served right out of the bowl with a handful of chips, this will find its way into your regular repertoire. The avocado adds a creamy richness that turns a simple salsa into a more complex condiment. Used sparingly on paper-thin tuna, this is an easy, elegant dish that doesn't require a lick of cooking, just a bit of slicing and some blitzing. *See photograph on page 36.*

4 medium tomatillos, husked and quartered

¼ small white onion

½ jalapeño

Good handful fresh cilantro, leaves and some stems

Juice of 1 lime, or to taste

Sea salt and freshly ground black pepper

1 avocado, halved and pitted

1 pound sushi-grade tuna, well chilled

Good-quality tortilla chips

In a food processor or blender, combine the tomatillos, onion, jalapeño, and cilantro and puree until smooth. Add the lime juice and season with salt and pepper. Taste and add more cilantro, lime, salt, or pepper as needed. Scoop the avocado into the tomatillo mixture. Puree until creamy.

Remove the tuna from the fridge and slice it against the grain as thinly as you can. To serve, lay the tuna on a plate and drizzle with some of the dressing. Serve with additional dressing and chips on the side.

crab, avocado, and black bean tostadas

GROWING UP IN SOUTHERN CALIFORNIA, WE ATE
Mexican food the way I imagine most families go through
mac and cheese. Whether it was the little white paper
dishes of tacquitos smothered in a lip-searing avocado
sauce that we'd make jaunts down from the Canyon to
Olvera Street to procure; the homemade tamales my
mother's friend would drop off, bundled in corn husks and streaking their brown bag
with clouds of grease; or the tostadas at Casa Mia (a dark but lively dive we frequented
just a stone's throw from the beach). Or my mom's own weekly conceit: homemade
salsa, guacamole, shredded cheese, sour cream, and warm beans spread across the
dinner table, tortillas steamed in foil and dealt like cards to each of us to fill as we saw
fit. All were standard and beloved fare from as far back as I can recall.

But perhaps the best was when we had company coming over and my mom was
going for a casual vibe. On those nights, she would up the ante on our make-your-own
approach by serving both a green and a red salsa, swapping in black beans for refried
(for some reason these seemed fancier), and dazzling guests with a brimming bowl of
freshly cracked crab. Whether other women were entertaining in this fashion I don't
know, but whenever company was mentioned, I hoped that one of my mom's luminous
Mexican dinners would follow.

I use the same trick today to keep dinner easy and a tad surprising: My only
refinements are quickly blitzing the beans with cilantro and lime in the food
processor to smooth them out, and tossing the crab with the avocado and chile so
there are fewer bowls on the table. Here's my suggestion: Serve these tostadas with
Avocado, As It Should Be (page 35), some grilled corn sprinkled with chili salt and
lime, and a dish of Pickled Red Onions (page 23), and graze away. You could also use
the tomatillo-avocado dressing (page 58) to brilliant effect. *See an additional photograph
on page 37.*

recipe continues

crab, avocado, and black bean tostadas

1 pound lump crabmeat

2 avocados

1 small Thai chile or ½ jalapeño, minced

Grated zest and juice of 2 limes, or more as needed

Sea salt and freshly ground black pepper

1 can (15.5 ounces) black beans, rinsed and drained

Good handful fresh cilantro sprigs, leaves picked (some stems are okay)

1 teaspoon ground cumin

Pinch cayenne pepper

8 or so corn tortillas, warmed (see Note)

A few radishes, sliced

Pickled Red Onions (optional; page 23)

Place the crab in a medium bowl, picking through lightly to make sure there aren't any bits of shell mixed in. Halve the avocados lengthwise and remove the pit. Run your knife lengthwise down the flesh of the avocados at ¼" intervals and then again crosswise so you have a relatively even grid. Using a soup spoon, scoop down between the skin and flesh and add the chunks to the bowl.

Add the chile and toss gently. Add the lime zest and half the lime juice and season with salt and pepper. Taste the salad and adjust the seasoning as needed. Set aside.

In a food processor, combine the beans, cilantro, cumin, cayenne, and the remaining lime juice. Puree until smooth, adding a bit of water if needed to achieve your desired consistency. Season with salt and more lime if needed. Transfer to a saucepan and keep warm over medium heat until the tortillas are ready.

To serve, spread some of the black bean mixture on each tortilla and then top with a scoop of the crab salad, a few sliced radishes, and pickled onions, if using.

Note: *Warm and lightly char the tortillas, one at a time, in a cast iron pan over medium-high heat, or bundle them in foil and warm in a 400°F oven while you make the beans.*

a bit of cooking

There are meditative moments to be found in the kitchen: the shelling of peas, the stirring of risotto, and the kneading of bread, to name a few. Activities that calm us down at the stove rather than wind us up. This section is laden with meditation-inducing dishes. Whether through the repeat piping of gougères, the delicate slicing of pears, the shaving of parsnips into ribbons, or the mustering of patience to slow-roast tomatoes, the dishes in this chapter make grazing simple, and they also make the act of cooking nourishing. I promise, nothing here requires much cooking, but the little you do will leave you happy you bothered.

roasted cherry tomatoes in olive oil

THERE ARE THINGS THAT YOU KNOW ABOUT YOURSELF, character traits (okay, flaws) that you have to work on constantly to keep at bay or under control because they are so deeply rooted in the core of what makes you, you. For me, one of these essential flaws is a deep and all-consuming lack of patience. I wasn't born with any. Not a lick. So when it comes to a recipe requiring a low oven temperature and a long, slow cooking time, I embrace it as an opportunity to become a better, more self-aware human being.

These tomatoes are part of my therapy. They are so good, so blissfully full of pure tomato-ness, and so useful as a condiment or small side dish that I make them regularly and have a batch in the freezer at all times. Take a deep breath and give them a couple of hours to bask in the warmth of a 250°F oven until they reach that heat-blistered, wrinkled, and weepily wonderful state. The long cooking time intensifies the quintessential sweet-tart-acidic flavor of either cherry or grape tomatoes, which in the dead of winter is a welcome treat when all you can find at the markets are those disappointingly anemic hothouse options. Served drowning in a puddle of extra-virgin olive oil along with a hunk of good hard cheese (pecorino is nice here) or a few disks of musky soppressata, these are well worth the wait. And coming from someone as impatient as I am, that means something. *See an additional photograph on page 108.*

2 pints cherry tomatoes on the vine or grape tomatoes, halved	**4–6 garlic cloves, smashed** **About ½ cup extra-virgin olive oil**	**Sea salt and freshly ground black pepper**

Preheat the oven to 250°F.

Arrange the tomatoes and garlic on a rimmed baking sheet. Drizzle everything with just enough olive oil to lightly coat. Sprinkle lightly with salt and pepper.

Roast the tomatoes until they are well shriveled but still juicy on the inside, about 2 hours. Remove from the oven and let cool a bit.

To serve, transfer the tomatoes to a bowl and cover in more olive oil. At this point, you can also add any other bits and pieces you like to the mix. To store, keep the tomatoes in olive oil and refrigerate or freeze.

provençal-style roasted nuts

ONE OF THE JOYS OF TRAVELING BACK TO SOMEWHERE you've been before is the sense of familiarity—the feeling that, while it's not your home, some part of that place *is* yours; you have a personal history there, a story all your own, however brief and fleeting it may have been. It's not unlike going to a restaurant on the first night of a trip and then returning again on the last night; you're not a regular, not a local, but for that last meal, you belong in a way you didn't just a few days before.

I've gone to Oaxaca a handful of times and each time I find myself sitting in the *zocolo*, the center of the town, at a small table outside one of the many restaurants, sipping a beer and eating dishes of salty peanuts spiked with a squeeze of fresh lime juice. The nuts have a burnt red papery skin that clings to your tongue, and they're smaller than the peanuts you get here—crunchier, too. The nuts in this recipe are different from those served at the cafes in the *zocolo*, but with a cool drink in hand, they bring back that feeling of being somewhere both foreign and familiar at the same time. Somewhere you belong, at least for right now.

2 cups nuts (half raw almonds and half walnuts, or any combination of nuts you like)

1 tablespoon unsalted butter

2 tablespoons honey

1 tablespoon light brown sugar

1 teaspoon sea salt

¼ teaspoon cayenne pepper

1 tablespoon finely chopped fresh rosemary

2 teaspoons fresh thyme leaves, chopped

Preheat the oven to 300°F. Line a rimmed baking sheet with parchment paper.

Place the nuts on the lined baking sheet and roast for 5 minutes. Turn them and cook until fragrant and lightly browned, another 5 minutes. Remove from the oven (but leave the oven on).

Meanwhile, in a small saucepan, combine the butter, honey, brown sugar, salt, and cayenne and stir constantly over medium heat until the butter has melted and the sugar and salt have dissolved. Remove from the heat and add the rosemary and thyme.

Pour the butter mixture over the nuts and toss well to coat evenly. Return the pan to the oven and continue roasting, tossing the nuts every 4 to 5 minutes, until golden and fragrant, 12 to 15 minutes. Let cool thoroughly. To serve, break up the nuts and transfer to a bowl.

trumpet mushroom chips

WHEN I TOLD MY FRIEND ERICA THAT I WAS ADDING mushroom chips to this book, she said, without missing a beat, "Please just don't call them vegan bacon." The hijacking of the roasted mushroom as a bacon replacement is irksome. It's not that I don't want vegans to have their crispy, salty, meaty fix; it's just that neither bacon nor mushrooms benefit from this linguistic co-opting. Bacon is undeniably delicious, but that doesn't mean its name should be bandied about freely as a moniker for anything salty and wonderful. Equally, mushrooms deserve the respect to be called by their rightful name, not treated as a stand-in for something off-limits to the animal-free among us. The implication is that mushrooms aren't quite up to snuff, but by re-labeling them, they might become a passable facsimile for something they are not. This is silly.

These chips are delicious because they are earthy in a way that pork isn't, toothsome in a manner that's very un-porcine, and beautiful in a way that even the best bacon cannot hope to be (I've never seen a piece of bacon shaped like a toadstool in the woods). These are roasted mushrooms dressed up with a bit of sweet and a bit of salt, all while maintaining their integrity. You can do this with any mushroom—shiitakes are smaller but also beautifully shaped and nice for an added crunch on salads (but please don't call them croutons). That said, the king trumpet (also called royal trumpet and king oyster) is my favorite because it has that whimsical, woodland silhouette that brings to mind a magical forest.

½ pound king trumpet mushrooms, cut lengthwise into ¼" slices

4 tablespoons extra-virgin olive oil

Sea salt and freshly ground black pepper

2 tablespoons soy sauce

1 tablespoon maple syrup

Preheat the oven to 300°F. Line two rimmed baking sheets with parchment paper.

Arrange the mushroom slices on the lined baking sheets in a single layer. Brush them with 3 tablespoons of the oil, using a pastry brush to coat evenly. Sprinkle lightly with salt and pepper. Bake for 30 minutes, then use a spatula to turn the mushrooms and bake until nicely browned and beginning to crisp on the edges, another 20 to 25 minutes.

Meanwhile, in a bowl, combine the soy sauce, maple syrup, and remaining 1 tablespoon oil.

Remove the mushrooms from the oven, brush lightly with the soy mixture, and return to the oven until they are nicely glazed, another 10 minutes. Serve hot.

pear crisps

TWO YEARS AGO KEN AND I DECIDED WE WANTED AN ORCHARD. Well, let me rephrase that: I was reading Nigel Slater's tome *Ripe* and was so smitten by his description of his damson plum tree that I decided I wanted us to have an orchard. Never one to trample my enthusiasm, Ken joined in and agreed we should plant a very small orchard. That weekend, after tearing up a patch of lawn for said orchard, we headed off to the nursery and returned with a dwarf peach, a Honeycrisp apple, a sour cherry, and a pear tree. That first year we admired our miniature orchard and hoped that in time it would bear fruit. This year, we were tickled to see that while the apple has yet to be pollinated, we had loads of fuzzy pinkish peaches and blushing green pears.

One day late in summer, I was heading to Rhode Island to pick Ken up from a work event and as I walked out, I stopped by the orchard to admire the bounty of pears, quietly envisioning all the tarts and crisps in my near future. When we got home the next day, I wandered over to once again count the pears and secretly compliment myself on this fruitful feat, when I realized the tree was bare. Seriously, not a pear in sight. I stood there, stunned and saddened, trying to figure out how, in less than 24 hours, all those glorious greenish-red gems could have simply vanished. It was then that I spied a squirrel high above in the oak tree staring down at me (I swear he was grinning). I called my mom to tell her of my defeat and all she said was, in a tone so matter-of-fact it would have made me laugh if I weren't near tears, "They must have been watching and waited until they saw you drive away." Sadly, I have yet to use my own pears, but I still make these crisps to serve with wine and cheese, a triple crème being especially decadent or a good bracing blue to soften the sweetness of the fruit.

4 firm pears, such as Bartlett

Preheat the oven to 250°F. Line baking sheets with parchment paper.

Use a mandoline or sharp knife to slice the pears lengthwise into very thin pieces. If you can, it's nice to keep the stem attached to a slice as you go.

Place the slices on the lined baking sheets and bake for 1½ hours. Flip the pears and continue to bake until they begin to turn golden brown on the edges, another 1 to 1½ hours. Remove from the oven and transfer to wire racks. The pears will crisp up as they cool.

ricotta-stuffed medjool dates wrapped (or not) in bacon

I LOVE THE WORD "MEDJOOL." IT SOUNDS LIKE SOMETHING out of the *Arabian Nights*, a single word that evokes richly colored silks, wrists draped in shimmering bangles, stiflingly hot souks, and tile-lined walls in every shade of blue. Supposedly it means "unknown." That alone is alluring, but evidently the fruit was so named because it came from a previously undiscovered date palm tree found in *an oasis in Morocco*. Seriously, how seductive is that? An unassuming wrinkled brown fruit found on an unknown tree discovered near a pool of crystal water in the midst of miles upon miles of dust storms and sand dunes—you can almost see Ingrid Bergman and Humphrey Bogart, dazzling in their crisp white linens, setting out on camelback to find this elusive spot and collect dates to take back to Rick's Café Américain, a treat to savor with their evening brandy. No, they don't look like much, but bite into one and taste that caramel sweetness and you'll be right there with me in my 1940s desert fantasy. Stuff these amber gems with milky ricotta to soften the honeyed flavor and then, if you feel inclined, wrap them in smoky bacon for a savory, succulent delight.

24 Medjool dates, pitted	½ cup fresh whole-milk ricotta cheese	12 slices thick-cut bacon (optional)
	Sea salt	

Preheat the oven to 450°F. Line a rimmed baking sheet with parchment paper.

Use a sharp knife to cut each date lengthwise down the middle, keeping the bottom intact. Fill a piping bag with the ricotta (or use a resealable plastic bag with the corner cut off). Squeeze a bit of cheese into the center of each date.

If you're not using bacon, bake the dates until they are warm and the cheese begins to soften, about 5 minutes. Sprinkle with salt and serve.

If you *are* using bacon, cut the slices in half crosswise. Wrap each date in a piece of the bacon and place them seam-side down on the baking sheet (if you'd like, you can run a toothpick through each date to secure them). Bake until the bacon begins to crisp on the edges, about 20 minutes.

Remove from the oven and serve.

creamy fava beans with olive oil and goat cheese

THERE ARE CERTAIN INGREDIENTS THAT intimidate me: Jerusalem artichokes, fiddlehead ferns, and cardoons come to mind. It's not that I don't love to eat them, but there's something about each of them that's standoffish to me as a cook. I've read recipes for them, but intuitively, I don't know what to do with them; they're so aloof, so much cooler than I am in the kitchen. I want to approach them, but they just seem out of my league. That's how it was for me with fava beans as well, until I had an escarole salad with fava beans and pecorino a few years back and decided I just adored favas too much to be so hesitant about approaching them. You know the issue: You have to shell them, blanch them, then peel them . . . they don't exactly make themselves easy to love. But I finally took a deep breath, gathered all the culinary confidence I could, and bought a bagful. And oh was it worth it. Once you break through that tough outer layer and start to see their tender, sweet, nuttier inside, you'll be smitten too—you just have to get to know them. Blitz them up with olive oil, tarragon, and some creamy goat cheese to serve on grilled bread or for dipping, and favas will be your new best friend, I promise. *See photograph on page 108.*

Sea salt

2½–3 pounds fresh fava beans, shelled (about 2 cups) or (even easier) 2 cups frozen shelled favas

¼–½ cup extra-virgin olive oil

½ small onion, chopped

Sea salt and freshly ground black pepper

1 sprig fresh tarragon, leaves picked

1 ounce goat cheese (about 2 tablespoons)

Bring a large pot of salted water to boil. If you're using fresh favas, add the shelled beans and simmer until they turn bright green, 2 to 3 minutes. Drain the beans and run under cold water to stop the cooking process and help keep their green color. Remove the outer peels and discard.

In a saucepan or skillet, heat 2 tablespoons of the olive oil over high heat. Add the onion and cook until tender and translucent, 3 to 5 minutes. Add the beans (freshly peeled or frozen, no need to thaw them first) to the pan and cook until tender, 1 to 2 minutes for fresh or 3 to 4 minutes for frozen. Season with salt and pepper.

Transfer the beans and onion mixture to a food processor, add the tarragon, and puree, adding some of the remaining olive oil through the feed tube as needed to achieve a thick but relatively smooth consistency. Finally, add the goat cheese and pulse again until just combined. Taste and adjust the flavors as you like—more tarragon, goat cheese, salt, or pepper.

blistered shishito peppers with flaky salt

THE RUMOR IS THAT FOR EVERY TEN SHISHITO OR padrón peppers, there's one in the mix that's fiery. I can tell you from personal experience that this is a myth. Sometimes I buy a bag at the farmers' market and not a single pepper sets my mouth on fire. Other times it seems as though every other one is a burning red ember destined to leave me reaching for a glass of water as my eyes tear up from the heat. The wonderful thing about this recipe is that the char you get on the peppers from the scalding cast iron pan masks the immediate burn of your tongue if you do get a hot one. And if you don't, well then you just get that wonderful char, followed by the piquant, grassy flavor of the pepper itself. Usually 2 to 3 inches in length, both shishito and padrón peppers are intensely green and furrowed with canyons that run the lengths of their skin, and while I tend to find shishitos more often in the market, either works perfectly. *See an additional photograph on page xiii.*

1–2 tablespoons extra-virgin olive oil	**1 pound shishito or padrón peppers**	**Flaky sea salt**

Heat a large cast iron pan over high heat. The pan should be large enough to hold all the peppers in a relatively even layer. If it isn't, cook in batches. Add enough olive oil to thinly coat the bottom of the pan and heat until just smoking. Add the peppers and cook, tossing frequently, until the skins begin to char and the peppers start to soften and wilt a bit, 3 to 4 minutes. Transfer to a bowl, sprinkle generously with salt, and serve.

sautéed sweet onion and chard toast with rustic tomme

I'M THE FIRST ONE TO ADMIT THAT CHEESE CAN be intimidating (see my full confession on page xxiv), but branching out beyond the old standbys is a low-risk adventure. A tomme, as I understand it on good authority, is the broad name for a group of small, roundish cheeses from the French or Swiss Alps that I find to be fruity and nutty with hints of salt. One of the most famous is the tomme de Savoie, though now some artisanal American makers are also producing tomme-esque cheeses that are well worth a gander. Find one you like and let this earthy combination warm the coldest winter day. Here's a thought: Light a fire if you have one, tug on the thickest of socks and softest of sweaters, and pair this toast with Sweet and Spicy Delicata Squash Crescents (page 89) and a cup of Potato and Leek Soup (page 88). Unless you're someplace warm—in that case, skip the socks and sweater and serve the soup chilled à la vichyssoise. *See photograph on page 147.*

2–3 tablespoons extra-virgin olive oil

1 large Vidalia onion or other sweet onion, very thinly sliced into half-moons

Sea salt and freshly ground black pepper

1 bunch green or rainbow chard, stems removed and cut into 1" ribbons

1 teaspoon sherry vinegar, or more to taste

Sliced rustic bread, toasted

Thinly sliced rustic cheese, such as tomme de Savoie, tomme crayeuse, or Consider Bardwell Manchester

In a medium saucepan, heat 2 tablespoons of the olive oil over medium-high heat. When the oil is hot, add the onions and sprinkle with salt and pepper. Reduce the heat to medium and cook, stirring frequently, until the onions begin to color, about 10 minutes. If the pan seems dry, add an extra tablespoon of oil.

When the onions are golden brown on the edges or even beginning to stick to the pan, stir in ½ cup or so of water and continue to cook until the liquid evaporates and the onions are very tender and have melded together in a tangle, another 10 to 15 minutes.

Add the chard leaves in batches until they begin to wilt, so they all fit in the pan, and cook, stirring occasionally, until just tender, 4 to 6 minutes. Add another tablespoon or so of water to soften the leaves, if needed. Add the vinegar, taste, and season again with salt and pepper, if needed. Remove from the heat.

Spoon the onion-chard mixture onto the toasts and, while still warm, top with the thinly sliced cheese—it will soften a bit as it sits on the hot vegetables.

prosciutto-wrapped grilled peaches with mint

SUMMER MAY OFFICIALLY START IN JUNE, BUT I never feel like it's really, truly summer until I bite into that first perfectly ripe peach. As much as tomatoes and cherries vie for the title of quintessential summer food, it's really this fuzzy, sunset-brushed stone fruit that's the bellwether for long lazy days and warm, firefly-sparked nights. With that in mind, we planted a miniature peach tree a couple of years ago and, as happened with our pear tree, the squirrels beat us to our glorious bounty. Or most of it. Having seen my beloved pear tree ransacked in a single night, I cleverly picked a handful of unripe peaches the next day, just in case those pesky garden thieves decided to hit the peaches next. Which of course they did. By the following week I had six or so rock-hard peaches in my fruit bowl and a woefully bare tree. But remarkably, the peaches I salvaged, while small, did soften, and they were everything one hopes for in a peach: the skin soft, downy, and fragrant and the flesh weeping with golden juices.

There's nothing like walking out and plucking a peach from your own tree . . . unless you have to do it preemptively to combat the local wildlife; then it's a little less romantic. So, forced to buy peaches for the rest of the summer, I asked the farmer at my local stand how he deals with the squirrel issue. He said, "Well, it's one of the less pretty parts of farming. We shoot 'em." I love peaches, I really do. But as a gardener, not a farmer, that's not something I'm okay with. In fact, I wished he hadn't told me so I could have at least enjoyed his peaches with a clear conscience. As for my crop, I've come to terms with sharing with the rest of the community. *See photograph on next page.*

4 peaches, quartered	8 slices prosciutto or other cured ham, torn in half	Handful fresh mint leaves
2 tablespoons extra-virgin olive oil		

Preheat a grill.

Lay the peaches cut-side up on a baking sheet and brush them with the oil. When the grill is hot, set the fruit cut-side down on the grate and cook for about 4 minutes or until grill marks appear and the fruit begins to soften. Flip the peaches and cook the other cut side until well marked as well. Remove from the heat and let sit until cool enough to handle.

Wrap each peach in a bit of prosciutto, scatter mint over top, and serve.

FOLLOWING PAGE: *Grilled Sardines with Meyer Lemons* (PAGE 103) | *Prosciutto-Wrapped Grilled Peaches with Mint* | *Persian Cucumbers, Snap Peas, and Red Onion with Lemon Zest* (PAGE 53)

roasted cherry tomato toast with brie and basil

WHEN I WAS A KID, MY PARENTS WOULD PULL US out of school for an extra week at the holidays so we could go to Europe when the flights were cheap. For us, off-season travel (meaning rainy and cold) was the norm; I assumed everyone headed to London in deepest December. But it was fun. We would rent a flat for part of the time (this was back before Airbnb or VRBO), buy a little Christmas tree that we'd decorate with ribbons from a local art shop, make a proper English roast with Yorkshire pudding, and my sister and I would worry like crazy that Santa wouldn't know we had left town and wouldn't be able to find us. Then we would head off to the countryside for a few days. I lost my dental retainer in a café in Bath once (we found it at the bottom of the very last garbage bag we dug through in the basement) and I learned my multiplication tables in a little town in Ireland called Blessington. Sometimes we'd drive, but more often we'd take the train, the best part of which was the café car. The idea of eating and watching the emerald green waves of farmland swoop by was just irresistible to my preteen eyes.

My favorite meal on these trips was a tomato and cheese sandwich on buttered white bread. Bought from a capped man behind the café counter, these sandwiches were cut into two triangles and sealed in a plastic box of the same shape. The cheese was a sharp white, the bread was soft and smeared from edge to edge with creamy yellow butter, and the tomatoes actually had flavor. I reckon I'd be disappointed if I bought this sandwich on a train today, but I've reimagined a version that reminds me of those travelers' lunches. Sure, this version goes a bit more Franco than Anglo, but the elements are all here.

About 24 cherry tomatoes	Sea salt and freshly ground black pepper	½ pound Brie, at room temperature
Extra-virgin olive oil	8 slices country bread	Fresh basil leaves

Preheat the oven to 400°F. Line a baking sheet with parchment paper.

Put the cherry tomatoes on the lined baking sheet and drizzle with olive oil. Roll the tomatoes around to make sure all are lightly coated. Sprinkle with salt and pepper. Roast until the tomatoes begin to soften and blister, about 20 minutes.

Turn the oven to broil. Brush the bread slices with olive oil, put them on a baking sheet, and toast until nicely colored, turning once to lightly crisp the underside as well. Remove from the oven and top each slice with slab of Brie. Drape a basil leaf or two over the cheese, top each toast with 3 or so roasted cherry tomatoes, and serve.

pimentón-spiced chickpeas with spinach and manchego on toast

THERE IS ALWAYS A CAN OF CHICKPEAS IN my cupboard, and here's why: Chickpeas are the superheroes of the pantry. Like the Wonder Twins, Zan and Jayna (remember them?), they can morph or transform into almost anything. Short on stuff to fill out a salad? Add a cup of chickpeas. Looking for an easy appetizer? Fry some chickpeas in olive oil and sprinkle them with sea salt and pimentón. Desperate for a quick stew? Toss a can of chickpeas on the stove with a can of tomatoes, a sausage or two, and some greens, and dinner is done. Tired of the same old pastas? Chickpeas with a bit of pancetta, Parmesan, and toasted breadcrumbs will do the trick.

Or, try this Spanish-inspired take on toast. The smashed chickpeas get tangled up in the garlicky spinach and it all takes on a notably smoky flavor from the pimentón and cumin. The creamy slivers of Manchego melt ever so slightly when they hit the hot legumes. It's a quick visit to Andalusia without ever leaving your kitchen. Serve this with Blistered Shishito Peppers with Flaky Salt (page 73), a dish of olives, and some extra Manchego for a simple, Spanish-inspired grazing meal.

2–3 tablespoons extra-virgin olive oil

1 garlic clove, minced

1 can (15.5 ounces) chickpeas, rinsed and drained

2 teaspoons pimentón (smoked paprika)

1 teaspoon ground cumin

Pinch red chili flakes

Sea salt and freshly ground black pepper

7 ounces baby spinach

12 slices rustic bread, brushed with oil and toasted

24 thinly shaved slices Manchego cheese

In a large skillet, heat 2 tablespoons of the olive oil over medium-high heat. When the oil shimmers, add the garlic and cook for about 1 minute or until fragrant. Add the chickpeas, pimentón, cumin, and chili flakes and cook until the chickpeas are warmed though, about 5 minutes. Season with salt and pepper. Gently smash the chickpeas with the back of a wooden spoon (you don't want them to become a paste, just broken down a bit).

Add another tablespoon of oil to the pan if it seems dry and add the spinach. Continue to cook, tossing frequently, until the spinach is wilted but not releasing too much liquid, about 1 minute. Remove from the heat and season again with salt and pepper.

To serve, generously scoop the spinach-chickpea mixture onto the toasts and top each with a couple slivers of shaved Manchego.

thyme-roasted parsnip tangle

I FEEL SORT OF BAD FOR PARSNIPS. I KNOW IT SOUNDS odd to empathize with a vegetable, but hear me out. They look like carrots, but are pale and more unassuming. They're not really eaten raw, so their utility is limited. They're often stumpy and squat, with a few warts and stray roots on display. They're not as well-loved as potatoes, not as bright and popular as carrots, not as exotic as celeriac, as bracing as turnips, as brilliantly colored as beets, or as precious as radishes, all decked out in shades of pink. The parsnip is, however, a delicious root vegetable that shines when treated well. Peeled into gossamer-thin strips, tossed with a bit of oil, cheese, and herbs, this wallflower becomes a willowy tangle of crispy ribbons. Like Eliza Doolittle breaking free of her Cockney accent and homely clothes to become a lady, with little more than a vegetable peeler, the overlooked parsnip can take your breath away, or at least tame your hunger.

3 parsnips, peeled

2 tablespoons extra-virgin olive oil

½ cup freshly grated Parmesan cheese, plus more for serving

3–4 sprigs fresh thyme, leaves picked

Sea salt and freshly ground black pepper

Preheat the oven to 400°F.

Use a vegetable peeler or mandoline to slice the parsnips lengthwise into long ribbons. This is easiest if you rotate the parsnip every few pulls, peeling evenly on all sides. Eventually you'll hit the core, which you can discard.

Transfer the ribbons to a baking sheet and toss them with the olive oil, Parmesan, and thyme and season with salt and pepper. Bake the ribbons, tossing every 2 to 3 minutes, until they are browned and crispy (they can color quickly on the edges if you're not paying attention), about 15 minutes. Serve hot with an additional sprinkle of cheese or thyme if desired.

classic croque-monsieur bites

YEARS AGO I WAS TRAVELING WITH A BOYFRIEND TO A close friend's wedding. The boyfriend should have been an ex already; I knew it before we left, but he didn't. I wanted to be heading to Paris with someone who made my insides melt when I caught his eye. I wasn't. After the flight, I remember being in the baggage claim area feeling ragged and drained. Standing there, waiting for our bags to tumble down the carousel, I saw another couple. They'd clearly been on our flight, but unlike us, they looked lovely; radiant and adoring, they were not off balance in the slightest.

She was tall and slim and moved like syrup, gracefully swaying as he held her from behind, his arms a cocoon around her waist. He had shaggy hair that wasn't simply unkempt from the flight; you could tell it was always that way, sexy rockstar meets seductive oil painter. I knew nothing about these two people except that they were happy. They were in France in the summer and they were about to embark on the trip I was craving so deeply. They would drink café au lait and eat croissants each morning feeling that fullness that only the prospect of an empty, idle day in a foreign city can elicit. They would wander aimlessly through cobblestone streets, stopping for drinks in an outdoor café whenever they felt like it; a Kronenbourg 1664 for him and a glass of Sancerre for her. They would share a croque-monsieur; a sandwich I'd never heard of before and would only discover on this trip.

The perfect combination of sharp Gruyère cheese, smoky ham, and butter-fried country bread makes for a sandwich that is complete, yet always seems to be leaving its mate behind on the menu. There's something sad about ordering the monsieur, delirious with anticipation for all that he offers, while thoughtlessly leaving the croque-madame behind. I guess I was in that kind of mood—the leaving kind. I broke up with that boyfriend the week after we returned (nothing ends an unhappy relationship faster than sitting through a happy couple's nuptials). But for years now, those two unknown lovers have stayed with me, a visualization of romance, travel, adventure, and love all bound up in a single embrace. Sometimes in airports I think of them: Are they still together? If I saw them at the baggage carousel now, would he still hold her just so? But then, and perhaps more importantly, my mind wanders to the love I discovered on that trip and I wonder: Will there be a really good croque-monsieur where I'm going now?

1 tablespoon butter,
plus more as needed

1 tablespoon all-purpose
flour

¾ cup whole milk

Pinch ground nutmeg

Sea salt and freshly
ground black pepper

2 tablespoons freshly
grated Parmesan cheese

1 cup finely grated
Gruyère cheese

4 slices rustic bread

Dijon mustard

¼ pound thinly sliced
Paris ham

Preheat the oven to 350°F.

In a saucepan, melt the 1 tablespoon butter over medium heat until just foamy. Add the flour and whisk until smooth, about 30 seconds. Gradually whisk in the milk, stirring constantly, until it thickens and nicely coats the back of a spoon. Remove from the heat, add the nutmeg, and season with salt and pepper. Stir in the Parmesan and 2 to 3 tablespoons of the Gruyère.

Butter both sides of the bread slices and toast in a skillet over medium heat until golden. Spread mustard thinly on one side of all the toasts. Dividing evenly, top two toasts with the ham and about ½ cup of the Gruyère. Top each sandwich with the remaining toasts, mustard-side in, and put on a baking sheet. Using a spatula or the back of a wooden spoon, spread the top of each sandwich with the béchamel sauce and sprinkle with the remaining Gruyère. Bake until the cheese begins to melt, about 5 minutes. Turn the oven to broil and broil the sandwiches until the top bubbles and browns, 2 to 4 minutes. Cut into squares and serve hot.

curried carrot and coconut soup

CURRY AND COCONUT CAN TRANSPORT ME FROM MY small apartment in the middle of the city to a land ablaze with golden minarets, silken dresses in every shade of the sunset, bejeweled women with hennaed hands, and hazy heat that blurs in the distance. No, I've never been there, but this is what I conjure when I stand in the kitchen pulling spices from the cabinet and opening a can of creamy, clotted-on-the-top coconut milk. The warmth of the spices and the tropical fruit blended with sweet carrots and ginger is both seductive and soothing—it's like curling up at home to read an E.M. Forster or Graham Greene novel on a rainy day. You get to disappear into another world, to float away to an exotic locale while feeling completely coddled at the same time. I tend to make this soup after I've bought a big bunch of carrots, only needing one or two. When those roots begin to taunt me from their drawer at the bottom of the fridge and threaten to go soft, I relent and treat us to this aromatic bisque.

3 tablespoons butter or olive oil

½ medium onion, roughly chopped

Sea salt and freshly ground black pepper

4 large or 6 medium carrots, chopped (4–5 cups)

1 piece (1") fresh ginger, peeled and grated

¼ teaspoon ground coriander

¼ teaspoon ground cumin

¼ teaspoon ground turmeric

Pinch cayenne pepper

¼–½ cup unsweetened coconut milk

Pinch sugar (optional)

Unsweetened coconut flakes (optional)

In a large saucepan, melt the butter over medium heat. Add the onion, sprinkle with salt and pepper, and stir to coat well with the butter. Cook until the onions are tender and translucent, 6 to 8 minutes. Add the carrots, ginger, coriander, cumin, turmeric, and cayenne. Stir and cook until the carrots are softened, about 10 minutes.

Add enough water to cover the vegetables by 1" (about 3 cups). Bring to a boil over high heat, reduce the heat to medium, and continue cooking until the carrots are cooked through, another 15 to 20 minutes.

Let the soup cool slightly. Working in batches if necessary, transfer the soup to a blender or food processor and puree until smooth. Blend in enough coconut milk to create the consistency you want. If it's still too thick after adding the coconut milk, loosen with a bit of water. Adjust the seasoning, adding the sugar to taste. If desired, serve garnished with coconut flakes.

spiced tomato bisque with goat cheese crumbles

TOMATOES AND CHEESE ARE A COMBINATION THAT works in so many forms. One of my favorite sandwiches is a version of tomatoes and cheese (page 78) adapted from the ones I enjoyed as kid traveling with my parents; there used to be a little restaurant down in SoHo called Salt that I would go to now and again for lunch, just to savor their sweet tomato soup served with melted Brie on a slice of baguette; and while I'm not one of them, I know many people who harken back to their childhood memories of being served Campbell's tomato soup with grilled cheese sandwiches on the side. I think it's the creaminess of the cheese—whether Brie, American, or otherwise—and how it smoothes out the acidic edge and the sometimes cloying sweetness of the tomatoes that makes it such a classic duo.

With this, one of my favorite winter soups, the same concept is in play. Using spice to bring out the savory side of the tomatoes (the ginger, cayenne, and chili flakes give it a kick that hints at the flavors of India without going the full distance), crumbles of creamy goat cheese are then swirled into the hot soup just before serving. This final ingredient leaves milky streaks, trails that cut through the hearty bisque, enriching the soup, blurring the heat, and offering up the occasional tangy crumb.

2 tablespoons extra-virgin olive oil	1 can (28 ounces) crushed Italian plum tomatoes	½ teaspoon red chili flakes, or more to taste
1 clove garlic, minced	1 cup water	Pinch cayenne pepper
1 piece (2") fresh ginger, peeled and grated	2 tablespoons sugar	4 ounces goat cheese, such as Vermont Creamery
1 cup diced onion	2 teaspoons fine sea salt	

In a large saucepan, heat the oil over medium-high heat until it shimmers. Add the garlic and ginger and sauté until just fragrant, 1 to 2 minutes. Add the onion and continue cooking until soft and translucent, about 5 minutes.

Add the tomatoes, water, sugar, salt, chili flakes, and cayenne. Reduce the heat to medium-low and simmer for 30 minutes to meld the flavors. Using an immersion blender, blender, or food processor, puree the soup until smooth. Add the goat cheese and stir well until the mixture is mostly combined with creamy streaks and a few evident crumbles of cheese. Ladle the soup into bowls to serve.

pea shooters with parmesan crisps

PARMESAN IS A BIT LIKE SEA SALT OR LEMONS TO me—it makes so many things taste more like they should. It certainly has its own potent personality, but when grated or shaved, it's like a soft whisper, an accent that elevates everything it touches. In this spring soup, the Parmesan is both a subtle seasoning and the only ingredient needed to make the delicate garnish served alongside said soup: a cheesy tuile—a savory brittle, a woven wafer. When fresh peas abound, this is a soup to serve chilled and enjoy with a glass of something cold on the patio. When the fresh peas are long gone but you're yearning to be reminded that the long winter days won't last forever, a box of frozen will do the trick—ladled up warm, it's a harbinger of longer, lazier days yet to come.

½ stick (4 tablespoons) unsalted butter, at room temperature

1 leek, cleaned and thinly sliced

2 cups fresh or frozen peas

3 cups chicken stock

1½ cups freshly shredded Parmesan cheese (use a coarse grater, not a rasp-style grater)

Sea salt and freshly ground black pepper

In a medium saucepan, melt 1 tablespoon of the butter over medium-high heat. Add the leek and cook until soft, about 5 minutes. Add the peas and swirl to coat in the butter, then add ½ cup of the chicken stock. Bring the stock to a simmer and cook for a minute or two, just until the peas turn bright green. Remove the pan from the heat.

Transfer the peas and their cooking liquid to a food processor or blender and puree. Add the remaining 3 tablespoons butter and ½ cup of the Parmesan and continue to process until smooth. Add the remaining 2½ cups chicken stock and process one more time until fully combined. Season with salt and pepper and set aside.

To make the crisps, preheat the oven to 375°F. Line a baking sheet with parchment paper.

Scoop tablespoon-sized mounds of the remaining 1 cup Parmesan onto the lined baking sheet and spread into rough 3" rounds, leaving at least 1" between them.

Bake until the cheese has melted and is lightly browned, 4 to 5 minutes. Remove from the oven, let the cheese just stop bubbling and set up a bit, and then lift the crisps from the parchment paper with a thin spatula. As they cool, the crisps will set up.

To serve, return the soup to the stove and heat. Pour the soup into shot glasses or small bowls and serve with the crisps.

potato and leek soup

EVERYONE HAS FAVORITE VEGETABLES, I IMAGINE. I'M PARTIAL TO artichokes, avocados, and leeks. There are, of course, many more on my list of loves, but those three are the first that come to mind.

Leeks are revelatory to me because of all they can do: They can be braised as a side dish, chopped and sautéed for a mirepoix, roasted in a gratin, grilled with little more than olive oil and salt and pepper, and, of course, blitzed up in soup. Their buttery, silky flavor reminds us that they're part of the onion family, but they're so much softer and sweeter. Unlike onions, shallots, or even scallions, leeks are not aggressive; they're never loud or brazen, even on their own. Leeks are demure, present but quietly so. But they can be frustrating too.

When you buy leeks, the ones you're hoping for are about a foot or more long, mostly white slender stalks with just a blush of a green neck that turns dark at the very top. But what you will often find are squat ones with less than an inch or so of creamy white stalk and a long, splayed pine green top. These are disappointing and should be left behind; the flavor is more forest-y than creamy and there's just not enough to go around. Especially in this simple soup, where you want at least two promising leeks, because contrary to what some might say, potato and leek soup should showcase both vegetables in equal measure.

½ stick (4 tablespoons) unsalted butter

2–3 leeks, cleaned and thinly sliced

2 russet (baking) potatoes, peeled and cut into chunks

Salt and freshly ground black pepper

4–5 cups chicken stock

¼–½ cup heavy cream or half-and-half

Chopped fresh chives

In a large deep saucepan, melt the butter over medium heat until the foam subsides. Add the leeks and sauté until very soft but not colored, 10 to 12 minutes. Add the potatoes and toss to coat in the butter. Season with salt and pepper and add enough stock to cover the vegetables by at least ½". Bring to a boil and then reduce to a simmer. Cook until the potatoes can be easily pierced with a knife, 12 to 15 minutes.

Working in batches if necessary, transfer the leeks, potatoes, and stock to a blender or food processor and puree until smooth. Return the mixture to the pan, add as much cream as you like, and taste for seasoning. Garnish with chives and serve with lots of good bread for sopping.

sweet and spicy delicata squash crescents

PROBABLY DUE TO NOTHING MORE THAN LACK OF imagination, I'd never made a Delicata squash until a couple of years ago. I had looked at them, noticing their slinky shape with just a shadow of a waist, admiring their sunshine yellow skin with rippling streams of green running down the outside, and thought about buying one.

But for some reason I didn't. Instead I returned to the known world of the kabocha and Hubbard, the oh-so-familiar land of the acorn and butternut. Until my pal Kate showed up to work one day with leftovers from the night before and offered me a taste. Kate and I work together quite a bit. We're both originally from Los Angeles, prefer being barefoot, could happily survive on cured meats, and think Negronis are the nectar of the gods. Suffice it to say, despite the crushing age difference that I choose to ignore and the fact that she has the kind of flaxen Breck Girl hair women kill for, I like her a lot.

So it was one of those slightly embarrassing but ultimately rewarding moments when I dipped into her Tupperware, tasted this wondrous squash, and had to acknowledge that I had been missing out on something special for way too long. Roasted with the skin still on, the ruddy orange slices were tossed with woodsy syrup and warm spices—and just enough cayenne and chili flakes to add a healthy kick of fire on the back end. Cut into little crescents that resemble waning moons, these will pair brilliantly with Roasted Brussels Sprouts with Pancetta and Maple Pecans (page 96) or Armenian-Spiced Baby Lamb Chops with Yogurt and Mint (page 107).

2 Delicata squash, halved lengthwise, seeded, and cut crosswise into ½"-thick crescents	**2½ tablespoons maple syrup**	**1 teaspoon red chili flakes**
2 tablespoons extra-virgin olive oil	**1 teaspoon ground cinnamon**	**¼ teaspoon cayenne pepper, or to taste**
		Sea salt

Preheat the oven to 400°F.

On a rimmed baking sheet, toss the squash with the olive oil, maple syrup, cinnamon, chili flakes, cayenne, and a generous sprinkling of salt. Make sure all the squash crescents are well coated and transfer the pan to the oven.

Roast the squash until they begin to brown on the edges, about 20 minutes. Use a spatula to flip the squash; they should release easily from the pan. If not, continue to cook for another 5 minutes or so, until they do. Cook on the second side until nicely colored and tender, another 10 minutes. Remove from the oven and transfer to a serving plate.

charred fava shells with lemon, chile, and anchovies

I DON'T GET HOME TO LA MORE THAN A FEW times a year, but whenever I do, a visit to Gjelina, the Venice restaurant that attracts Angelinos and tourists alike, always gets squeezed in. It's the first stop my parents and I make on our drive home from the airport for lunch, the place we go for one nice dinner, or, as happened last time, the quick bite I grab on my way back to the airport when I'm jumping on a red-eye.

I was home not too long ago for work and after a full week of shooting, my assistant Kate and I were bound for that last flight out after a long day. With barely 2 hours to kill and a rental car to return, we looked at each other and silently agreed to make a beeline for Gjelina, grab a quick dinner at the bar, and still make the 10:30 p.m. Virgin America back to New York. We found a parking spot right out front (the gods were on our side), grabbed stools, and ordered a silly amount of small plates and a pizza.

All was good, but the one dish I couldn't shake, the one that I had to deconstruct so I could recreate it for Ken the following night, was this one. Fava beans served in their pods (I had never considered such a thing), grilled and marinated in some lemony-garlicky brew. Back in New York the next evening, while still a bit groggy but before I could lose the thread, I picked up some tender favas (small and young is what you want), pulled out my cast iron pan, and took my best guess at the marinade. This is what I came up with; but since they weren't on the menu the next time I was there, I have no idea if my memory served me well or not. Let's pretend it did.

recipe continues

charred fava shells with lemon, chile, and anchovies

¼ cup extra-virgin
olive oil

2 garlic cloves, smashed

Grated zest and juice
of 1 lemon

3–4 anchovy fillets

1 teaspoon red chili
flakes

Sea salt

1 pound small young
fava beans in their pods

Thinly shaved
Parmesan cheese

In a bowl large enough to hold the beans, combine the olive oil, garlic, lemon zest and juice, anchovies, and chili flakes. Mash up the anchovies with a fork and combine all the ingredients well. Taste, decide if you need salt (the anchovies may be enough), and let sit to macerate while you cook the beans.

Set a cast iron pan over high heat or light a grill. If you're using a cast iron pan, keep the heat relatively high and lay the favas in the dry pan in an even layer. If you're using a grill, turn the heat to medium and lay the favas so they won't fall through the grates.

Cook the favas, turning as needed so they char in spots but don't burn, about 10 minutes total. You want the favas to color on the outside but also cook through—ideally, the outside pod will soften and the inner beans will steam.

When the beans are lightly charred and very soft, transfer them to the bowl with the marinade and let sit for 15 minutes or longer—the more time they rest in the marinade, the more they will absorb the flavors. To serve, transfer to a large dish and garnish with shavings of Parmesan. Then eat them, pod and all, before they disappear.

roasted beet tartare with cheese and pistachios

THERE ARE A LOT OF PEOPLE WHO WILL SAY that roasted beets and cheese (most often goat cheese) is passé, that it should be retired as a culinary concept. I will admit that restaurants might have gone a little overboard with the beet and goat cheese salad at one point in time, but no one ever gave such strife to the sudden ubiquity of tuna tartare or the everywhereness of kale salad. Popular combinations can, like anything, become classics or clichés. Either way, if they taste good, who cares? I came to beets late in life. Beyond the bottle of borscht my dad kept in the fridge to soothe his nostalgic cravings, we didn't eat beets much when I was a kid. And even though I have always been someone who will happily consume almost anything set before me (what Laurie Colwin so aptly called "a kind of universal recipient—the O-positive for hostesses"), when I first tasted beets, they brought to mind sweetened dirt. I was unconvinced.

For quite some time, when asked what I didn't like, there was one ruddy-colored root that always came to mind. But exactly what drove other more high-minded and haughty eaters away is what drove me toward them; roasted beets with goat cheese were everywhere—I couldn't escape. It was like they were taunting me, daring me to dismiss them over and over again. So I relented; a girl can only be so mean for so long. They were still sweet, and now they were earthy (that was probably the dirt-thing from way back when). Some were the savagely burgundy-stained ones I had long avoided, but others were a sunny golden hue. Served with two small disks of lightly crumb-crusted and fried chèvre over a bed of citrus-dressed arugula, they humbled me.

I've now been eating beets for years and I don't care what anyone says—roasted beets are illuminated when paired with a creamy, tangy, buttery cheese. Instead of the traditional goat, I like La Tur, a luscious Italian number made from cow, sheep, and goat's milk that's oozy and silken at the same time. If you want to stay slightly more classic, try Coupole, a triple crème goat's milk cheese from Vermont Creamery.

recipe continues

roasted beet tartare with cheese and pistachios

3 medium beets

1 shallot, very finely minced

3 tablespoons extra-virgin olive oil

1–2 tablespoons fresh orange juice, or to taste

Sea salt and freshly ground black pepper

½ cup raw pistachios

1 round triple crème cheese, like La Tur or Coupole

Fresh mint leaves (optional)

Preheat the oven to 400°F.

Cut the tops off the beets, leaving about 2" of stem (this helps keep them from bleeding as they cook). Wrap each beet completely in foil and place them on a baking sheet. Transfer to the oven and roast until a sharp knife easily pierces the vegetable, about 1 hour depending on size. Remove the beets from the oven and let cool.

Meanwhile, in a small lidded jar, combine the shallot, olive oil, orange juice, salt, and pepper and shake to combine. Set aside.

When the beets can be handled, remove the foil, trim the tops and bottoms, and peel (some people like to use gloves or paper towels for this, as beets can stain your hands). When the beets are totally peeled, use a mandoline or sharp knife to slice them into thin rounds.

Lay the beets in an overlapping fashion on a platter, drizzle with the dressing, and sprinkle with the pistachios and mint, if using. Serve with the cheese.

roasted brussels sprouts with pancetta and maple pecans

INTERSTATE 5, THE HIGHWAY THAT runs through the Central Valley of California, isn't the most romantic of roadways, but for me it holds a sense of dusty nostalgia—a wide, flat expanse of blacktop pummeled by big-rig trucks and pickups, dust kicking up behind wheels, and sprinklers the size of airplane wings dousing the acres of fields that line both sides of the road. My memories of that drive consist of searing hot days, the windows of our Volvo station wagon open to hair-dryer hot gusts, and the mountains off in the distance wobbling in a watery yellow sky.

But what I recall even more vividly is the sulfurous smell of the various crops that would envelop the car at certain points along the way: the powerful aroma of cabbage, broccoli, and Brussels sprouts, the perfume of our state's industry and identity. For miles at a time, the entire car would be suffused by the smell of agriculture. To this day when I find Brussels sprouts, usually only in the fall, I buy them on the stalk—there's a Zen to be found in popping off one at a time into a waiting bowl, and the pungent smell is a quick, nostalgic jaunt back to those drives up the spine of my home state.

1 cup pecans

1 tablespoon unsalted butter

1 tablespoon maple syrup

½ teaspoon sea salt, plus more to taste

1 tablespoon extra-virgin olive oil

¼ pound pancetta, cut into ¼" dice

1 pound Brussels sprouts, trimmed and quartered

1 tablespoon sherry vinegar, or more to taste

Preheat the oven to 400°F.

Spread the pecans on a baking sheet and roast until fragrant, 4 to 5 minutes.

In a small saucepan, melt the butter, then stir in the maple syrup and salt. Pour the butter mixture over the hot nuts and toss to coat evenly. Set aside.

Meanwhile, in a large saucepan, heat the olive oil over medium-high heat. Add the pancetta and cook, stirring occasionally, until the fat has rendered and the pork is just beginning to color, 8 to 10 minutes.

Add the Brussels sprouts to the pancetta and cook until the sprouts are bright green and crisp-tender, 3 to 4 minutes. Season as needed with salt, add the vinegar, and toss well to combine. Toss with the reserved pecans and serve.

moroccan spiced carrots

I DON'T KNOW A LOT OF PEOPLE WHO WON'T EAT A RAW carrot. The cooked carrot, however, is another story. For every person who likes cooked carrots (I count myself among that group), there always seems to be someone who pushes them off to the side of their plate, like a child sent to the corner for misbehaving.

I think one reason many people don't like cooked carrots is because they've only eaten bad ones—or to put it more delicately, overcooked ones. An overcooked carrot loses its sweet character and turns mealy, torpid, and depleted. A properly cooked carrot—braised, grilled, roasted, or sautéed—maintains a subtle rigidity right at the core; whether the exterior is expertly charred or gently glazed, the inside maintains a tender structure with soft, nutty, caramel-y notes. With a properly cooked carrot, you can still taste the essence of earth, and you know that what you're eating was once rooted in fertile and damp soil. The only trick to cooking perfect carrots is pulling them out of the oven or off the heat when a sharp knife inserted into the thickest part pierces the flesh but meets with a bit of resistance (for a lot of us, that means 10 to 20 minutes earlier than usual). Shower your carrots in a medley of Moroccan-inspired spices, douse with a bit of citrus, and cook until just tender—with this approach, even dissenters will likely be swayed.

3 bunches baby carrots or small carrots (rainbow are nice)

3 tablespoons extra-virgin olive oil

1 teaspoon ground cinnamon

1 teaspoon ground cumin

½ teaspoon ground coriander

½ teaspoon red chili flakes

Pinch cayenne pepper, or more to taste

Sea salt

Grated zest and juice of 2 lemons or 2 oranges

Preheat the oven to 400°F.

Peel the carrots and trim their stems to about ½", leaving a bit of a handle at the top.

Put the carrots on a rimmed baking sheet and drizzle with the olive oil. Sprinkle the carrots with the cinnamon, cumin, coriander, chili flakes, and cayenne and season with salt. Toss to coat evenly. Roast until the carrots are just beginning to caramelize and color, about 15 minutes. Shake the carrots around on the pan and let them cook until just tender, another 5 to 10 minutes.

Remove the carrots from the oven, sprinkle with the lemon zest and juice, and transfer to a serving plate. Serve warm or at room temperature.

farmers' market gratin

MY IDEA OF A GRATIN INCLUDES PRETTY MUCH anything I can top with breadcrumbs mixed with Parmesan cheese. I'm partial to wide, low baking dishes or pans so that you get as much surface area for the breadcrumb mixture as possible (as with a crumble, that's the part everyone really wants anyway). When I first started making this gratin, which is pretty much an everything-in-the-kitchen-sink vegetable casserole, I made it in a rather extravagant way and saved it mostly for company. It was certainly impressive, but it was also a bit of a chore. I would slice all the vegetables and roast them individually, drizzled with olive oil and sprinkled with salt and pepper, in single layers on individual baking sheets until they were tender and just brown. This took some time. After they cooled I would layer them, one vegetable at a time, in concentric circles in a springform pan, pressing down after each layer. Then I would bake the final terrine, because that's basically what it was, until the breadcrumb topping was golden and the vegetables were warmed through. Releasing the vegetables from their spring-loaded corset revealed a many-layered torte that captured the flavor of late summer.

Then one day Ken said, "Why don't you just toss them all together raw and bake them without all the fuss—wouldn't that work?" "I suppose it might," I responded, finding his casual tone and cavalier idea somewhat irksome and wondering why it hadn't occurred to me before. So now I slice, toss, and layer them loosely (not lavishly), adding the breadcrumbs halfway through the baking so they don't brown too fast. It's not as stunning in terms of presentation, but it takes a fraction of the time and effort, which is really more suited for a late-summer dish anyway.

Extra-virgin olive oil, as needed

1 large Vidalia or other sweet onion, halved and thinly sliced

2 garlic cloves, roughly chopped

Sea salt and freshly ground black pepper

1 medium eggplant, cut crosswise into ¼"-thick disks

2 medium zucchini, cut into ¼"-thick disks

2 yellow summer squash, cut into ¼"-thick disks

3 Roma (plum) tomatoes, cut into ¼"-thick disks

4–5 sprigs fresh oregano or thyme, leaves picked

2 cups homemade breadcrumbs

1 cup finely grated Parmesan cheese

¼ teaspoon red chili flakes

In a large pan over high heat, add enough olive oil to generously coat the bottom, 2 to 3 tablespoons. When the oil shimmers, add the onion and garlic, sprinkle with salt and pepper, and reduce the heat to medium. Cook, stirring frequently, until the onion begins to color, about 10 minutes. If the pan seems dry, add an extra tablespoon of oil.

When the onions are golden brown on the edges or begin to stick to the pan, stir in ¼ cup or so of water and continue to cook until the liquid evaporates and the onions are very tender and have melded together in a tangle, another 10 minutes. Set aside.

Preheat the oven to 375°F.

Meanwhile, in a large bowl, toss the eggplant, zucchini, and summer squash with enough olive oil to coat everything lightly (½ cup or so). Sprinkle with salt and pepper and toss again. In a large, wide gratin dish—round, oval, or rectangular—begin layering the vegetables so they partially overlap like fish scales: Start with a layer of eggplant, then zucchini, summer squash, and then tomatoes. Drape half of the caramelized onions over the tomatoes, sprinkle with some of the herbs, and repeat the layers again. Don't worry if you're short on some of the vegetables; just keep working until all are used up.

Transfer the dish to the oven and bake until the vegetables become tender, release their juices, and brown a bit on top, about 45 minutes.

Meanwhile, in a medium bowl, combine the breadcrumbs, Parmesan, and chili flakes with a few good glugs of olive oil. Season with salt and pepper and toss to combine.

Spread the breadcrumb mixture over the partially cooked vegetables and return the dish to the oven. Cook until the top is nicely golden and bubbling at the edges, another 10 to 15 minutes. Remove from the oven and serve hot or at room temperature.

spanish-style shrimp with chile

KEN AND I HAD LANDED IN SEVILLE ON AN unexpectedly chilly November afternoon. Delivered by a taxi that rumbled along the curvy cobblestone streets, we arrived at our hotel, an old mansion right in the center of the town, and found ourselves in a high-beamed room with embroidered cotton sheets on the bed and wide clay tiles on the floor. Upon opening the window, we were met with a horizon line of rooftops, stucco in every color from putty to persimmon. The crisp air wafted in, carrying with it the scent of Seville oranges and helping us bat back the fatigue that lurked behind our eyes.

A quick shower and change of clothes later, we set out in search of that odd-houred meal travelers always seem to need: the one too late to be lunch but far too early to qualify as dinner, especially in a country where they don't even leave the house before 8 in the evening. Wandering the narrow alleyways that constituted streets, we found our way to a bar. Amber-colored hams with glossy black hooves dangled from a rack above, and a thick potato-filled *tortilla*, slices already missing, sat on the counter and beckoned us to stay a while. With glasses of woodsy red wine before us, we ordered a half *ración* of the local Ibérico ham, a slice of the *tortilla*, and a dish of *gambas al ajillo*—sweet, garlicky, smoky shrimp that arrived in a low terra-cotta dish, the olive oil still bubbling like liquid gold. With a basket of warm bread for sopping and a dish of buttery green olives, this was the post-flight, pre-adventure, midday grazing meal we needed.

4 garlic cloves, peeled

20–24 medium shrimp, peeled and deveined

½ cup extra-virgin olive oil

Sea salt and freshly ground black pepper

½ teaspoon pimentón (smoked paprika)

Generous pinch red chili flakes

1 teaspoon sherry vinegar

2–3 sprigs fresh Italian parsley, leaves picked

Rustic bread

Grate the garlic into a bowl large enough to hold the shrimp. Add the shrimp and ¼ cup of the olive oil, season with salt and pepper, and let sit for 15 minutes or so.

When you're ready to cook, in a large skillet, heat the remaining ¼ cup olive oil over high heat. When the oil is hot, add the shrimp, grated garlic, and any oil in the bowl along with the pimentón and chili flakes. Cook, tossing and stirring constantly, until the shrimp are pink and just cooked through, about 3 minutes. Add the vinegar and toss to combine. Garnish with the parsley and serve with the bread for sopping up any juices.

asian-inspired crab cakes with soy-lime dipping sauce

A GOOD CRAB CAKE CAN BE HARD TO FIND. THE ONES YOU get at restaurants tend to be loaded with more mayonnaise and breadcrumbs than crab, which of course is not the point; a really good crab cake should be mostly crab. Or in this case, mostly crab with a bit of shrimp. The shrimp does two jobs here: First, it gets blitzed up to act as the binder (no mayo needed), and second, its sweet flavor enhances the crab so you find yourself with a turbo-charged crab cake, the oceanic shellfish flavor boosted rather than muted. Dressed up with traditional Asian flavors (chile, scallion, cilantro, and ginger), these are not the crab cakes your guests are expecting. I make these quite small—only a couple of inches in diameter, as they really are the epitome of finger food.

6 medium shrimp, peeled and deveined

1 teaspoon Thai fish sauce

1 pound lump crabmeat, picked over for shells

1 large egg

¼ cup chopped scallion

¼ cup chopped fresh cilantro

1 small fresh chile, minced

1 teaspoon minced fresh ginger

¼ cup homemade breadcrumbs

Sea salt and freshly ground black pepper

¼ cup soy sauce

Grated zest and juice of 2 limes

1 tablespoon toasted sesame oil

¼ cup peanut or vegetable oil, plus more as needed

½ cup all-purpose flour

In a small food processor, puree the shrimp until you have a smooth paste, then add the fish sauce. Transfer to a medium bowl and add the crab, egg, scallion, cilantro, chile, ginger, and breadcrumbs. Season with salt and pepper and refrigerate for about 30 minutes so it's easier to handle.

Meanwhile, in a small bowl, combine the soy sauce, lime zest and juice, and sesame oil. Whisk well and set aside.

When the crab mixture is stiff enough to handle, shape into small disks about 2" in diameter; return the cakes to the fridge for a few minutes to set up again.

In a large skillet, heat the peanut oil over high heat. When the oil shimmers, dredge the cakes in the flour. Fry the cakes, reducing the heat as necessary to prevent burning, and turning once, until nicely browned on both sides, about 8 minutes total. Serve with the dipping sauce.

grilled sardines with meyer lemons

I SPENT A WEEK ONCE WITH MY FRIEND JACKIE toodling around Corsica, a small French island in the Mediterranean off the coast of Nice, a stone's throw from Sardinia. A craggy, mountainous place, Corsica harbors flavors of both the countries that shoulder it, yet it has a rustic individuality all its own. Our first day on this island, we headed down the thread-thin coastal road that skims Cap Corse, en route to a place we'd read about in the guidebook called the Les Calanques de Piana. Not sure what to expect, we were riveted by the eroded granite rocks that spun skyward out of the earth and down into the sea below, a ragged wall of crag that changed color as the sun moved, appearing a rich salmon pink one moment, then burnt clay the next. Transfixed by Mother Nature's architecture, we decided to stay in Piana, winding our way to the sole hotel in town, a sweeping palace of a place called Hôtel Les Roches Rouges. This grand arch-windowed and column-laden structure was perched on the edge of a cliff, the wide terrace hanging precariously over the sea. It was a bit down at the heels, a shadow of what it must have been at one point, but stunning nonetheless.

When we arrived, a few older men sat drinking Pernod in the sun, women in floppy hats sipped the local pink wine, and Jackie and I pinched ourselves for having stumbled into something out of another time. That first night, in a dining room that harkened back to days when people dressed for dinner, we shared the bouillabaisse as the waiter had recommended. It was so salty as to be almost inedible, so we ate the bread and drank wine instead. The next day, being a few hours wiser, we ate at a beachside restaurant, sharing more of the pink wine along with a salad of green beans, tomatoes, and hard-boiled egg, a generous wedge of the local sheep's milk cheese, and a platter of perfectly grilled sardines, just pulled from the sea. *See photograph on page 76.*

¼ cup extra-virgin olive oil

Grated zest and juice of 2 Meyer lemons, plus 4 whole Meyer lemons

8 whole fresh sardines, cleaned, head and tails removed if you prefer

Sea salt and freshly ground black pepper

Heat a grill or grill pan until very hot. In a small bowl, mix the olive oil and lemon zest and juice together and brush over the sardines. Season with salt and pepper.

Halve the remaining 4 lemons. When the grill is hot, add the fish and lemon halves, face down. Cook the fish until nicely lined on both sides and cooked through, 3 to 4 minutes per side. Cook the lemons until well charred. Serve the sardines with the charred lemons for squeezing.

summer spiced crab cakes with basil aioli

BEFORE WE EMBARKED ON BUYING OUR PERPETUAL fixer-upper of a cottage in Connecticut, Ken and I used to rent a small place every summer on the coast of Rhode Island. A little Craftsman, it sat on a shimmering cobalt lake just a stone's throw from the front patio. By walking down across the grass and through a forest of rhododendrons, all tortured and bent to form a shadowy tunnel, you were led to a dock adorned with nothing more than two Adirondack chairs, our annual beacon after a year in the city. Creatures of habit that we are, each year we would arrive, drop our stuff, and head to the local market for provisions so that we could spend at least the next day not having to leave the lake if we so chose. Beyond the local corn, tomatoes, fish, and Brickley's chocolate almond and coconut ice cream, we also always procured a pound of fresh crab. As was our habit, the next day we would make these Old Bay–spiked crab cakes for lunch, an unstated declaration that yes, we were officially on vacation.

1 pound lump crabmeat, picked over for shells

4 scallions, minced

3 sprigs fresh cilantro, leaves picked and chopped

1½ teaspoons Old Bay seasoning

¼ cup homemade breadcrumbs

¼ cup mayonnaise

Sea salt and freshly ground black pepper

1 large egg, plus 1 large yolk

½ cup extra-virgin olive oil

1 tablespoon Dijon mustard

Juice of ½ lemon

2 teaspoons white wine vinegar

Good handful fresh basil leaves

¼ cup vegetable oil, or more as needed

½ cup all-purpose flour

In a bowl, combine the crab, scallions, cilantro, Old Bay, breadcrumbs, and mayonnaise. Season with salt and pepper. Add the whole egg and mix gently. Divide into patties, about 3 ounces each. Chill until set and easy to handle, about 30 minutes.

While the cakes chill, in a blender or small food processor, combine the olive oil, mustard, lemon juice, vinegar, egg yolk, and basil. Puree until very smooth, then taste and season with salt and pepper. Set aside.

In a large skillet, heat the vegetable oil over medium-high heat. Dredge the cakes in the flour. Reduce the heat to medium and fry the cakes until nicely browned, about 3 minutes per side. Serve with the basil aioli.

lemon-tarragon chicken skewers

KEN AND I ONCE SPENT A YEAR LIVING IN A SMALL town on the coast of Connecticut. We rented an old house with a garden and a slim view of the water, and in the evenings, we'd watch the gulls dip and dive over the sailboats. We idled as the sun slipped away, watching as the light turned to a watercolor wash of pink and blue, the shade that colors the insides of seashells and only seems to happen by the ocean.

At the time, we were not only discovering the pleasures of living at the beach, but also attempting to be gardeners. Among our early efforts was an herb garden, or what I liked to think of as an herb "walk," as we had planted a variety of different herbs alongside a path we cut near the vegetable patch we'd started (we were naively ambitious with our early adventures). This walk was no more than a collection of mismatched flat stones we'd found in the shed and laid to create a footpath, but my hope was that the herbs would take off and the whole length of stones would have that rambling lush but manicured English garden effect.

That didn't quite work out as I'd envisioned, but the rosemary, oregano, and mint did run wild in the sea air. Sadly, the tarragon never really flourished; instead, it crept slowly along, providing just enough for me to continually clip off the leggy strands, pluck the silken leaves, and use it for cooking. With this tender, licorice-flavored herb on hand, one of our favorite dinners was chicken marinated in lemon and tarragon. Barely a recipe, I know; it's more a suggestion for marrying flavors meant for one another.

¼ cup extra-virgin olive oil

Juice of 1 lemon

1 small bunch fresh tarragon, leaves picked and chopped (about ¼ cup)

1 pound chicken tenders (or breasts cut lengthwise into 1"-thick strips)

Sea salt and freshly ground black pepper

At least 1 hour before you want to cook, in a wide baking dish or bowl, combine the olive oil, lemon juice, and tarragon. Add the chicken, season generously with salt and pepper, and toss well to combine. You want the tarragon to really stick to the meat. Cover the dish with plastic wrap and refrigerate for at least 1 hour or up to 8 hours.

When you're ready to cook, remove the chicken from the fridge and let it come to room temperature while you heat a grill or grill pan to high.

Thread each piece of chicken lengthwise onto a skewer. Cook until grill marks appear on both sides and the chicken is cooked through, 5 to 7 minutes total. Transfer to a serving platter.

armenian-spiced baby lamb chops with yogurt and mint

I FOUND A SLIM, RED, SPIRAL-BOUND cookbook at a thrift shop once called *Treasured Armenian Recipes*. It was from the early '70s, and it caught my eye because a friend of Armenian descent had recently thrown a cocktail party and had made a platter of baby lamb chops that were ridiculously good. The recipe, she said, was her mother's. When I found the little book, I thought it would be fun to give to her, but upon showing it to her, she said, "That's the book my mom cooks from. I have it." And so I kept it. It's one of those old community cookbooks, a collection of recipes handed down from cook to cook.

About the same time I found this book, my dad mentioned one he'd recently read—*Passage to Ararat* by Michael Arlen, which traces a son's journey back to Armenia to discover what his father and family left behind when they emigrated to the States. I immediately bought it. And while this recipe isn't adapted from either of these books, it is inspired by both. *See photograph on next page.*

2 tablespoons cumin seeds

1 tablespoon fennel seeds

1 tablespoon coriander seeds

1½ teaspoons sea salt, plus more as needed

1 tablespoon freshly ground black pepper

2 garlic cloves, finely minced

Extra-virgin olive oil

12 lamb rib chops

1 cup whole-milk Greek yogurt

Grated zest and juice of ½ lemon

2 sprigs fresh mint, leaves picked and chopped

Combine the cumin, fennel, and coriander seeds in a mortar and crush well with a pestle (or put them in a small plastic bag, seal, and smash with a rolling pin or the bottom of a pan). When the spices are well combined, transfer them to a small bowl and add the salt, pepper, garlic, and enough olive oil to make a loose paste.

Heat a grill pan or grill until very hot. Rub the lamb chops evenly with the spice paste, coating both sides of each chop well. Cook the chops until grill marks appear and the meat releases easily, about 5 minutes. Turn the chops and cook for another 2 to 3 minutes for medium-rare. Remove from the heat and let rest.

In a bowl, mix the yogurt, lemon zest and juice, mint, and salt to taste. Serve the chops with the yogurt on the side.

FOLLOWING PAGE: *Roasted Cherry Tomatoes in Olive Oil* (PAGE 64) | *Creamy Fava Beans with Olive Oil and Goat Cheese* (PAGE 71) | *Zucchini Ribbons with Herbed Goat Cheese* (PAGE 55) | *Armenian-Spiced Baby Lamb Chops with Yogurt and Mint*

worth the effort

The beauty of grazing is how easy—or involved—it can be. There is a time and place for the simple antipasti, ingredients rummaged from the fridge and pantry and set on a board strewn with well-chosen cheese and charcuterie. And then there are the times when you want to make something that requires a bit more energy, something that demands rolling or kneading, some slow simmering or deep frying. For those days, when you want to get lost in the kitchen for a while and emerge with fat-topped jars of pâté or cups of soothing stew, these are your recipes.

red onion and raspberry jam

"HAVE I TAUGHT YOU NOTHING?" HE SAYS TO ME, MAYBE halfway in jest, as he resets my grip. Yes, I have already forgotten what I've spent the better part of 20 years learning—in yoga, when you bind in side angle pose, the wrist of the hand wrapping around your back should be gripped by the hand scooping up from under your ribcage. The idea is to open your shoulder by pulling down, not up. I know this in my head, but my muscle memory is lacking sometimes, or maybe it's my focus that's wobbly, or my ever-present impatience that's throwing me off. No matter, with his light touch, my patient teacher corrects me—again. I've been practicing yoga for a long time now, but I am still no closer to conquering flying crow or a forearm stand than I was on day one. Yet I keep trying.

Cooking is a lot like yoga. It's as much about the process as the final product; it's about being as present at the stove as you are at the table. There's a soul-soothing peacefulness in the kneading of bread, a healthy degree of focus needed to not burn nuts or overcook an egg, and yes, a Zen calm to be captured in the repetitive slicing of onions. All these little tasks are part of daily practice, part of what makes being in the kitchen so worthwhile—these acts force me to connect with myself in a way that matters, regardless of what the outcome is.

This jam is a practice in kitchen yoga for me because every step requires some patience, focus, and repetition. The slicing of the red onions into slender half-moons, sweating them slowly until they begin to wilt as though exuding a deep sigh of exhaustion, and then, the continued stirring of the pot until a rich magenta tangle that's both tart and sweet begins to emerge. It's an excuse to let everything else around you vanish for a bit (the process), while also creating a delicious condiment that makes almost anything it touches taste better (the outcome). I like to think of it as onion jam pose. *See photograph on page 117.*

| ¼ cup extra-virgin olive oil | 2 large red onions, peeled and cut into thin half-moons | Sea salt |
| | | ¼ cup raspberry vinegar, or more to taste |

In a large skillet, heat the olive oil over medium-high heat until shimmering. Add the onions, sprinkle with salt, and reduce the heat to medium-low. Cook, stirring occasionally, until they are very soft but not coloring, 10 to 15 minutes.

Add the vinegar and continue to cook, stirring, until the onions begin to break down and meld together, another 20 minutes or so. Taste and adjust the seasoning, adding more vinegar or salt if needed. When the onions are the consistency of jam, remove them from the heat, let cool completely, and transfer to an airtight container for up to 2 weeks.

flaky cheddar biscuits with heirloom tomatoes and peaches

WHEN JULY AND AUGUST, AND YES, EVEN SEPTEMBER come around, I do as little cooking as possible—it's more about picking and choosing, slicing and chopping, a bit of grilling and a lot of sipping. Because when the farmers' market is overflowing with tomatoes of every kind and baskets of fuzzy, lusciously ripe peaches abound, the cook becomes sort of irrelevant. Which is why I have the good sense to do nothing more than gather up a bagful of each and obey as these strong-willed and sensual orbs beg me to let them live together in some manner of mingling.

Some days, when it's just a couple of us and everyone is happy to grab a fork and dip into the same bowl, I'll roughly chop up the tomatoes and peaches and toss them with slivered red onion and cilantro, dousing it all with lemon juice for a rustic salad. But when Ken has his way, both fruits are sliced and slipped into the middle of a freshly baked tender cheddar biscuit. Flaky, buttery, and rich, these mottled biscuits absorb all the soft, honeyed juices of the peaches while the dewy seeds from the tomato cling to the crumb. Think of it as sweet-and-savory shortcake, if you will.

1½ cups all-purpose flour, plus more for dusting

2 teaspoons baking powder

½ teaspoon baking soda

½ teaspoon sea salt

1 cup finely grated sharp cheddar cheese

½ stick (4 tablespoons) cold (or better, frozen) unsalted butter

1 cup heavy cream

2 large heirloom tomatoes, sliced

2 large peaches, sliced

Preheat the oven to 425°F. Line a baking sheet with parchment paper.

In a large bowl, combine the flour, baking powder, baking soda, salt, and cheddar. Using the large holes of a box grater, grate the butter into the bowl. Using your fingers, blend the mixture together until it resembles coarse meal—be sure not to overwork the mixture; some larger pieces of butter are fine.

Add the cream to the bowl and mix until thoroughly combined. Transfer the dough to a lightly floured work surface and pat into an 8" round. Use a 2" to 3" biscuit cutter to cut into biscuits and transfer to the prepared baking sheet. Gather the scraps, pat out, and cut more biscuits.

Bake the biscuits until lightly browned and puffed, about 15 minutes. Let cool for a few minutes, then split the biscuits horizontally and fill each with a slice of tomato and a few peach slices. Top with the remaining biscuit half and serve immediately.

creamy chicken liver pâté with (or without) red onion and raspberry jam on brioche

IN MY VERY EARLY 20S, WHEN I FIRST STARTED trying to cook dishes I thought of as sophisticated and worldly; when I began spending Saturdays making the Silver Palate's coq au vin, Julia Child's *boeuf bourguignon*, and Time-Life's cannelloni; long before culinary school; back when my idea of becoming a good cook meant tackling recipes demanding complicated trussing techniques and cheesecloth-bound bundles of fresh herbs, I knew that pâté had to work its way into my repertoire. Luckily, I was also smart enough to know that good pâté is all about the sweet, fatty flavor of the livers, accentuated but not overwhelmed by other ingredients.

This is my idea of a perfect pâté: onions and butter and thyme and brandy and cream and lots of freshly ground pepper all blitzed up to bring out the best in the livers (and if you happen to have duck instead of chicken on hand, all the luckier for you). I think you'll find this is sublime smeared on brioche (or anything, really), but I can't help suggesting you top it with a tiny bit of Red Onion and Raspberry Jam (page 112) if you have it. *See photograph on page 117.*

1 stick (8 tablespoons) unsalted butter, at room temperature

1 onion, chopped

1 pound chicken livers

Sea salt

⅓ cup heavy cream

1 tablespoon fresh thyme leaves

Freshly ground black pepper

2–3 tablespoons brandy

1 loaf brioche bread

Red Onion and Raspberry Jam (optional; page 112)

In a medium skillet, melt 2 tablespoons of the butter over medium-high heat. Add the onion and cook until softened but not coloring, about 4 minutes. Add the livers to the pan, sprinkle with salt, and cook until the livers begin to brown, about 3 minutes. Flip and cook on the other side. You want the outside to brown but the inside to stay relatively pink. If you're not sure about how the livers are cooking, cut into one and check.

Transfer the livers, onion, and all the buttery juices to a food processor. (Reserve the skillet.) Add 4 tablespoons of the butter, the cream, thyme, and a good bit of pepper to the processor and puree until smooth.

Add the brandy to the skillet you fried the livers in and set it over high heat to deglaze and cook off some of the alcohol. Then add the brandy to the puree and pulse a few times to combine.

Set a fine-mesh sieve over a large bowl. Pour the liver puree into the sieve (you may have to work in batches depending on the size of your sieve) and use a rubber spatula to press the mixture through the sieve. Then do it again—I know it's a pain, but it's worth it for a truly perfect pâté without a hint of any grainy bits. Once the mixture is velvety smooth, transfer to a wide-mouth jar. Smooth the top.

In a small pan, melt the remaining 2 tablespoons butter over low heat and spoon off any foam. Pour the melted butter over the top of the pâté (this will keep the livers from discoloring), cover, and refrigerate to set up, ideally overnight.

To serve, cut the brioche into ¼"- to ½"-thick slices and halve on the diagonal. Toast until the slices just begin to color.

Remove the hardened butter seal from the top of the pâté and smear each toast with a bit of the pâté (once the butter seal is broken, you can keep the pâté sealed in the jar for a couple days).

Serve the pâté with the brioche toasts and, if desired, top with a bit of Red Onion and Raspberry Jam.

duck rillettes on toast

THIS IS MY HOLIDAY GO-TO, PARTY-PLEASING CULINARY COUP.
Rillettes and pâté are those homemade treats that people seem to think are really difficult to make, when in fact they're not. With the advent of really good duck confit now available in most decent grocery stores (or easily ordered by your butcher), you don't need to buy a whole duck and spend 2 days making the confit in order to make rillettes (yes, another shortcut, but one I'm not even a little embarrassed to take). My friend Daniel taught me how to get the consistency of rillettes just right by using the paddle attachment on my stand mixer. The paddle gently breaks down the meat and perfectly creams it with the rendered fat. I've added the zest and juice of a clementine (you can use any sweet citrus, but come Christmas, the time of year I'm most driven to make rillettes, those squat spheres, the smallest of the mandarins, always seem to be lurking in the fruit bowl as symbols of the season, so why not?), lots of fresh thyme, a splash of brandy, and just a hint of Dijon mustard. Decadent? Definitely, but that's the point. Don't forget the Champagne.

2 duck legs confit

¼ cup softened duck fat, plus more as needed

3–4 sprigs fresh thyme, leaves picked

Grated zest of 1 clementine or other small orange, plus 1 tablespoon juice

1 teaspoon Dijon mustard

1 teaspoon brandy

Sea salt and freshly ground black pepper

Baguette, sliced and toasted, for serving

Remove the meat from the duck legs, separating any excess fat and discarding the bones. (I save the fat to melt down for frying potatoes and use store-bought fat for the rillettes, as the 2 duck legs don't usually provide enough.)

Transfer the meat to a stand mixer fitted with the paddle attachment. Add the duck fat and mix on medium speed until the meat begins to shred, about 2 minutes. Add the thyme, clementine zest and juice, mustard, and brandy and continue to mix until the meat is finely shredded and fully combined with the fat; it should be spreadable in consistency. If you want it creamier, add a bit more fat, but go slowly, as it can get too fatty. Season with salt and pepper, taste, and adjust the seasoning as needed.

Transfer the rillettes to an airtight jar, pack tightly, and smooth the top. Melt an additional tablespoon or so of duck fat over low heat and pour the fat over the top of the rillettes to create a seal. Cover the jar and keep refrigerated; serve with toasts.

ALSO PICTURED: *Chicken Liver Pâté with (or without) Red Onion and Raspberry Jam* (PAGE 114), *bottom right* | *Red Onion and Raspberry Jam* (PAGE 112), *left center*

herb-scented gougères
(aka cheesepuffs)

KEN AND I WERE DRIVING AROUND BURGUNDY A FEW YEARS
ago. We were en route to meet my parents in Paris for a week
and decided to tack on a few days in the region where some of
our favorite wines are made. Our first stop was just outside
Chablis, where a Dutch couple had renovated a magnificent old
estate and turned it into a quietly elegant hotel with acres of
vegetable gardens, fruit orchards, horses, cows, chickens—well, you get it. Being off-
season, we happily found that we had the place to ourselves; it was as though this
sprawling and enchanting spot had been reserved just for us to wander and discover
without a trace of humanity beyond the owner trimming his hedges off in the distance,
two setters swirling madly around his boots.

After a long walk and a short nap, the owners kindly invited us to join them for an
aperitif. While we both tend to avoid socializing when traveling, and were sufficiently
jet-lagged to have legitimately said no, we were swayed by the dreamy quality of the
day. Wandering down to what they misleadingly called the lounge—a stone room the
size of a barn with 20-foot sliding glass doors left open to the courtyard beyond,
meticulously decorated in French chic with a fireplace tall enough for me to stand in—
we found flutes of the local bubbly and our hostess's homemade gougères awaiting.
The fizz from the wine went right to our time-addled heads, but the buttery golden
puffs of *pâte à choux* were sobering. These little puffs of pastry were crisp on the outside
with a soft, custard-like bite and just a whisper of cheese. Full of air, they teased and
left us wanting more. So I couldn't help but try and recreate them for us back at home.
Of course, it's hard to replicate something you've tasted so briefly, no matter how you
try to memorize the texture and flavor; it's often not the recipe but the experience as a
whole that you're craving . . . but it's always worth a try.

1 cup water	1 cup all-purpose flour	3 sprigs fresh thyme, leaves picked
1 stick (8 tablespoons) unsalted butter, cut into small pieces	4–5 large eggs	
½ teaspoon sea salt	1½ cups finely grated Parmesan cheese, sharp white cheddar cheese, or a mix	

Preheat the oven to 400°F. Line two rimmed baking sheets with parchment paper.

In a large saucepan, combine the water, butter, and salt and bring to a boil over high heat. Reduce the heat to medium so the mixture simmers. Add the flour and cook, stirring constantly with a wooden spoon, until the mixture pulls away from the sides of the pan, about 2 minutes.

Remove the pan from the heat and cool for a few minutes (you don't want the mixture so hot that the eggs begin to cook when you add them). Add 1 egg at a time, beating well after each addition, until you've added 4 of the eggs. Every time you add an egg, the dough will seem to separate, but it will come back together as you beat. You want the batter to be very shiny and smooth, and it should fall in slow ribbons from your spoon. If the batter seems too stiff, beat the remaining egg in a small bowl and add it, a spoonful at a time, while continuing to stir until you reach the desired consistency. When the dough just holds soft peaks and falls nicely from the spoon, stir in the cheese and thyme.

Fill a pastry bag fitted with a ½" plain tip with the dough and pipe out 1" rounds on the lined baking sheets, leaving an inch or so between them. Bake for 15 minutes, then switch the position of the baking sheets. Bake until the gougères are puffed and beginning to color and crisp (they should sound hollow when tapped on the bottom), another 15 minutes. Remove from the oven and turn off the heat.

Being careful not to burn yourself, use a skewer or sharp paring knife to make a small hole or cut in the bottom of each gougère and return them to the oven for another 5 minutes (this will allow the inside to crisp a bit and prevent deflating). Serve hot.

spanish tortilla with sweet onion and thyme

IT DOESN'T HAPPEN VERY OFTEN, BUT EVERY NOW and again I wake up in the middle of the night starving, ravenous, aching for a meal like I haven't eaten in days, as though I hadn't just had dinner a few hours ago. This hunger is strange because it feels so pure, so much like true hunger, not the "it's time for dinner" kind of hunger or the "I haven't eaten for a few hours so I'm peckish" post-lunch sort, but the kind that leaves your insides waning, your stomach physically tugging inward. It's the kind you experience after a long-haul flight (altitude always leaves me hungry) or following a day at the beach, caressed by the sun and water, your body depleted by the elements and desperate for something to restore it. When I get this strange nocturnal longing for food, what I want is very specific: a slice of Spanish *tortilla*.

Appropriately enough, I first tasted a Spanish *tortilla* in Spain, but since then I've eaten them almost solely in the comfort of my own kitchen. Through my research and various trials and errors, I discovered that the secret to a transcendent *tortilla* is the largely overlooked step of soaking the cooked potatoes in the egg mixture for at least 15 minutes before beginning to fry the final dish. By soaking the softened potatoes and onions, you allow the flavors to meld and the potatoes to absorb some of the egg— it makes all the difference.

My own addition to the *tortilla* (which actually wasn't my idea at all, it was Ken's) is fresh thyme; the thyme is not classically Spanish, but it adds an intoxicating smokiness that's worth the tinker with tradition. I must confess though, I have yet to satisfy my midsleep cravings. Instead I turn over, gently nudge Ken awake, and report, "I'm starving." His very reliable response is to pull the pillow over his head and mumble something other than what I long to hear (which would be, "Oh my beloved! Let me get up and make you a *tortilla*!"). So I go back to sleep, my mind adrift with thoughts of tender potato tangled up with sweet onion, all bound together in an eggy embrace. *See photograph on page xiii.*

½ cup olive oil, plus more as needed

1 large sweet onion, thinly sliced

Salt and freshly ground black pepper

3–4 sprigs fresh thyme, leaves picked

3 medium russet (baking) potatoes, peeled and very thinly sliced

6 large eggs

In a 10" nonstick skillet, heat ¼ cup of the olive oil until it shimmers. Add the onions and sprinkle with salt and pepper. Reduce the heat to medium-low and cook until they begin to soften and color, 10 to 15 minutes. Add the thyme and stir to combine.

When the onions are tender and golden, add the potatoes and continue cooking over medium-low heat, tossing frequently so all the slices are coated in oil. The pan will seem very full, but don't worry; as long as the potatoes have a chance to become partially cooked, it's fine. Continue tossing them every couple of minutes so they all have a chance to cook, about 20 minutes total. As you stir the mixture, be careful: You want to keep as many of the potatoes intact as possible to get a nice layered effect in the finished *tortilla*.

Meanwhile, in a large bowl, beat together the eggs and season with salt and pepper.

Remove the potato-onion mixture from the pan and let it cool slightly (you don't want it so hot that it cooks the eggs), then add it to the egg mixture. Gently toss to combine, and then let sit for about 15 minutes, so the potatoes absorb some of the eggs.

Add the remaining ¼ cup olive oil to the pan and heat over medium-high heat until quite hot (it's important to get the oil hot so the eggs seize up and form a nice crust). Carefully pour the egg and potato mixture into the pan, spread it around evenly, and cook for about 1 minute; reduce the heat to low and cook until the underside and edges of the *tortilla* are set but the top is still loose and jiggly, about 15 minutes. Shake the pan to loosen the *tortilla*, using a spatula if necessary. Slip the *tortilla* out, cooked-side down, onto a plate as large as the pan.

Place another plate of the same size on top of the *tortilla*, flip it over, and slide it back into the pan, cooked-side up. Continue cooking the *tortilla* over low heat until it's fully set and moves around easily in the pan, another 10 minutes. Once it's finished cooking, invert the *tortilla* again.

Cut the *tortilla* into slices and serve right away, or wait an hour or so. It may sink a bit in the middle, but the flavors will meld together and taste even better when served at room temperature.

a trio of tartlettes
(smoked salmon & asparagus, prosciutto with tomato & basil, and crab with tarragon)

ONE OF THE BEST MEALS I'VE EVER EATEN IN Paris didn't involve a trendy bistro or a traditional brasserie, but a last-minute shopping trip. Ken and I landed, napped, and headed out into the bitter cold November afternoon in search of all things French. By the time we headed back to the little apartment we had rented with a view of the Eiffel Tower, lit up and sparkling like the bubbles in a glass of Champagne, it was nearly 6 in the evening—on a Sunday. And, though we'd been duly warned by friends, we didn't totally absorb the reality that most of Paris closes down on Sunday evening and feeding yourself can be close to impossible if you haven't planned accordingly. Realizing the error of our ways, we dashed into the only open patisserie we could find and were lucky enough to procure their sole remaining chicken and leek quiche, a jar of vegetable soup, and an apricot tart. We went home, drank the wine our host had graciously left, and ate our picnic staring out at the Tower, happier than I can explain.

The variations I have here are some of my favorites, but you can use almost anything you like or have left over in the fridge—instead of buying smoked salmon or crab, feel free to use up those extra sautéed mushrooms, handful of baby spinach, or bit of roast chicken. Think of this crust-and-custard combination as a blank canvas for what you have on hand that sounds good to you.

PASTRY
1 stick (8 tablespoons) cold unsalted butter, cut into ½" pieces

1¼ cups all-purpose flour

¼ teaspoon sea salt, plus more to taste

¼–½ cup ice water, more or less as needed

CUSTARD
2 large eggs

⅓ cup whole milk

⅓ cup heavy cream

Sea salt and freshly ground black pepper

SMOKED SALMON & ASPARAGUS FILLING
1 slice smoked salmon, torn into small pieces

3–4 asparagus spears, trimmed and shaved into ribbons with a peeler

Goat cheese, for topping

PROSCIUTTO, TOMATO & BASIL FILLING
1–2 slices prosciutto, torn into small pieces

2 slices Roma (plum) tomato

¼ cup freshly grated Parmesan cheese

4 or so fresh basil leaves, for topping

CRAB & TARRAGON FILLING
½ cup lump crabmeat, picked over for shells

¼ cup grated Gruyère cheese

3–4 sprigs fresh tarragon, leaves picked

recipe continues

a trio of tartlettes

To make the pastry: In a food processor, combine the butter, flour, and salt and pulse until the mixture resembles coarse meal, about 10 pulses. Slowly add ¼ cup of the ice water through the feed tube and pulse until the mixture begins to come together, forming a dough. If you need to, add more water, 1 tablespoon at a time, and pulse again. Stop the machine and dump the mixture onto a clean work surface.

Bring the dough together with your hands and knead once or twice until it forms a ball—don't worry if it's not totally uniform; you should see patches of butter in places for a flaky crust. Form into a disk, wrap in plastic wrap, and refrigerate for at least 30 minutes.

Remove the dough from the fridge. Dust a clean work surface with flour, unwrap the disk, and use a rolling pin to roll it into a 15" × 10" rectangle. Cut the dough into six 5" squares. Press the dough evenly into the bottom and up the sides of six 4" tart pans. Trim the edges and prick the bottom of the crusts lightly with a fork. Freeze or chill the tarts for at least 30 minutes.

Preheat the oven to 375°F.

Meanwhile, to make the custard: In a large bowl, whisk together the eggs, milk, and cream. Season with salt and pepper.

Once the crusts are very cold, gently place a piece of foil inside each tart shell, making sure it's snug against the edges, then weigh the foil down with pie weights or beans. (The weights will keep the bottoms from puffing up and the edges from sliding down.)

Put the tart pans on a baking sheet and bake until just beginning to color on the edges, 10 to 12 minutes. Remove from the oven, carefully grasp the edges of the foil, and lift the weights and linings from the pans. Return the tart shells to the oven until the bottom crusts look dry, another 3 to 5 minutes. Remove the tart shells from the oven and reduce the temperature to 350°F.

Divide the custard mixture among the tart shells, filling them no more than two-thirds of the way full. Top two of the tarts with the smoked salmon, asparagus ribbons, and a crumble of goat cheese. Top another two with the prosciutto, a slice of tomato, the Parmesan, and a bit of basil. Top the final two with the crab, Gruyère, and tarragon leaves.

Bake until the custard is set, 20 to 25 minutes. Serve hot or at room temperature.

braised leeks with lemon-dijon vinaigrette

THERE'S A TINY LITTLE RESTAURANT IN LONDON called Casse-Croûte on Bermondsey Street (I love saying that: Bermondsey), just around the corner from Borough Market, one of my very favorite outdoor food markets. Casse-Croûte is a mouse hole of a place with just a few tables that are all within knee-knocking distance of one another. It has a very limited and ever-changing menu, and is that rare thing: a French restaurant so good and so authentic, you actually feel like you're in France. When I was there recently, I was seduced, as I usually am, by the starters more than the main courses (though the roasted John Dory did look quite amazing), and ordered the first thing on the chalkboard: a soft-boiled egg with a very small slice of smoked haddock over braised leeks.

The egg was miraculous. It was not only soft-boiled to perfection, but it was served whole and out of the shell; I'd never seen such a thing. A wiggly white orb that proved perfectly cooked when pierced, the tangerine-toned yoke spilling out onto the leeks and haddock, softening the richness of the hollandaise bath that all the ingredients waded in. The leeks were astonishingly tender yet still attached right at the root, reminding me of a well-poached artichoke heart in terms of texture. I've brightened up the sauce, making it a simple vinaigrette, and skipped the haddock, but let me say this: A dish of soft-boiled eggs and a plate of some smoked fish would fill out this grazing meal beautifully.

3 tablespoons unsalted butter	Sea salt and freshly ground black pepper	Grated zest and juice of 1 lemon
4 large leeks, white and light green parts only, cleaned and cut into 4" lengths	½ cup chicken stock 3 tablespoons extra-virgin olive oil	1 tablespoon Dijon mustard

In a large, lidded skillet, melt the butter over medium-high heat. When the butter foams, add the leeks and season with salt and pepper; reduce the heat to medium and sauté until they start to become tender, about 5 minutes. Add the stock, bring to a simmer, and cover. Cook until the leeks are very soft, another 15 to 20 minutes. Remove the lid, increase the heat, and cook until the liquid reduces and thickens. Remove from the heat.

In a small bowl, combine the olive oil, lemon zest and juice, and mustard. Whisk well to combine and season to taste with salt and pepper.

When you're ready to serve, transfer the leeks to a platter and drizzle with the vinaigrette. Serve hot or at room temperature.

barely-battered squid with old bay mayo

SQUID CAN BE SCARY IF YOU'VE NEVER cooked it before. The raw, dare I say slimy, texture is obviously a deterrent for some, and with those coil-like tentacles freckled violet on one side and lined with tiny suckers on the other, well, the otherworldliness can curb one's desire to get too close. Certainly the idea of cleaning the translucent eight-armed critters can prove a nonstarter for the squeamish among us. But try and clear your mind of all this for a minute. Think instead about how much you love a lightly battered, perfectly fried, salt-dusted, lemon-doused plate of calamari. Imagine you're sitting by the sea with a glass of straw-colored wine in your hand when suddenly, the beautiful server with the long dark hair and cocoa eyes (man or woman, you choose) sets down a dish of this squid before you. How great would that be? And it could totally happen. However, if it seems far-fetched, here's my thought: Ask your kind fishmonger to clean and cut up the squid for you, so all the dirty work is done.

Olive oil, for deep-frying

1 cup mayonnaise

3 tablespoons Old Bay seasoning

1½ pounds cleaned squid, sliced into rings, tentacles halved lengthwise if large

Sea salt and freshly ground black pepper

1 cup all-purpose flour

1 cup whole milk

Lemon wedges, for serving

Pour 2" of olive oil into a deep pot and heat over medium-high heat to 350°F (use a candy thermometer) or until a pinch of flour sizzles when added to the oil.

While the oil heats, in a bowl, combine the mayonnaise and 2 tablespoons of the Old Bay. Refrigerate until it's time to serve.

Pat the squid dry with paper towels and season well with salt and pepper. Put the flour in a wide bowl and season with the remaining 1 tablespoon Old Bay. Add the milk to a second wide bowl.

When the oil is hot, working in batches, dip the squid in the milk, dredge in the flour, shaking off as much excess as possible, and then add to the oil. Fry the squid until it just begins to color, about 3 minutes (don't overcook, or it will get tough). Use a slotted spoon to fish out the squid and transfer to paper towels to drain. Sprinkle immediately with a bit more salt, if desired, and repeat with the remaining batches. Serve with the Old Bay mayo and lots of lemon wedges.

ALSO PICTURED: *Crispy Asparagus and Shallots* (PAGE 128)

crispy asparagus and shallots

I HAVE NOT EATEN AT STATE BIRD PROVISIONS IN SAN Francisco. I hope to, I want to, I plan to, but I haven't yet. I actually have to admit that I had never heard of State Bird until I was lucky enough to style a *New York Times Magazine* piece that featured some of the dishes from the restaurant. If you're like me and haven't heard of it, it's a highly acclaimed spot serving Western-style food in a dim sum fashion: think trollies careening between tables laden not with pork buns, but with delicate plates of fried spears like these, their outsides crisp with just a shadow of the green asparagus gleaming through the crust. At least that's how I imagine it, not having been myself. This recipe being an adaptation of an adaptation, I can't promise that these will live up to expectations if you have been lucky enough to eat there, but I can say they're delicious. I skip the fried scallions used in the original recipe in favor of shallot rings; my dipping sauce is simplified; and I favor an irregular mix of breadcrumbs, some the size of sand and some of small pebbles, the variation giving each spear a ragged, rustic crust. *See photograph on page 127.*

1 garlic clove, peeled

4 anchovy fillets, or more to taste

¼ cup extra-virgin olive oil

Grated zest and juice of 1 lemon

Freshly ground black pepper

Olive oil, for deep-frying

2 large eggs

2 tablespoons heavy cream

Sea salt

2 cups all-purpose flour

2 cups homemade breadcrumbs, not too fine

1 bunch asparagus, trimmed

2 shallots, sliced into ¼" rings

½ cup shaved Parmesan cheese

On a cutting board, mash and then roughly mince the garlic clove with the flat side of a large knife. Add the anchovies to the garlic and mince together a bit, then use the side of the knife to mash them into a cohesive paste. Transfer the paste to either a small jar with a lid or a bowl and then add the extra-virgin olive oil, lemon zest and juice, and a generous grind of pepper. Shake or whisk to combine. Taste and adjust the seasoning as needed.

Pour about 1" of olive oil into a large, deep pot and heat to 350°F (use a candy thermometer) or until a sprinkle of flour sizzles when added to the oil.

While the oil heats, in a wide bowl, mix the eggs and cream together and season with salt and pepper. Put the flour in a second wide bowl and the breadcrumbs in a third.

When the oil is hot, dredge the asparagus spears in the flour first, then the egg mixture, and finally the breadcrumbs. Working in batches so you don't overcrowd the pan (and in turn lower the temperature of the oil), add the asparagus. Cook until each spear turns a rich, golden brown, then transfer to paper towels to drain. Once all the spears have been fried, repeat the dredging and frying with the shallot rings.

Serve the asparagus scattered with the shallots, topped with shavings of Parmesan cheese and a bowl of the dipping sauce.

asparagus and herb frittata bites

WHEN I GRADUATED COLLEGE, I WENT TO LONDON WITH dreams of cooking. (I ended up waitressing, but that's another story.) As a 21-year-old on a very limited budget, my desire to immerse myself in the burgeoning British food revolution was quelled by my pocketbook. Instead, I found myself eating regularly at a bustling restaurant near where I was staying. This lively (and largely youthful) spot had three essential things going for it: The staff didn't mind how long you sat at your table with a book, the wine was cheap, and they made a fantastic omelet, a dinner perfectly suited to my alone-in-a-foreign-country state of mind and budget.

For a few pounds, I could sit and read (I was deep into Virginia Woolf's *The Voyage Out*), feel terribly sophisticated sipping from a stout globe of claret-colored wine, and fill my belly with a cumulus of buttery eggs, sharp but silken cheese, and vegetables. The omelets weren't the slim sheath-like rolled sort you find in France—these were lush golden nests with dimples of brown butter on the skin and creamy curds emanating from within, which is what I lust after in an omelet or frittata. I prefer frittatas these days; they're easier (no turning) and you get more of that custardy layer on the top. With spring asparagus and chives (or tarragon if you're feeling saucy), this is the centerpiece of a grazing breakfast, lunch, or dinner. And it goes without saying that I hope you take liberties with the vegetables, cheese, and herbs as you see fit.

2–3 tablespoons extra-virgin olive oil

1 medium leek, cleaned and very thinly sliced

Sea salt and freshly ground black pepper

About 12 medium asparagus spears, cut on the bias into 1" pieces

6 large eggs

2 tablespoons heavy cream or milk

2 tablespoons chopped fresh tarragon or chervil

¼ cup goat cheese

8–12 fresh chives or handful fresh tarragon leaves

Preheat the broiler.

In a 10" ovenproof nonstick skillet, heat the olive oil over medium-high heat until it shimmers. Add the leek, sprinkle with salt and pepper, reduce the heat to medium, and cook, stirring occasionally, until very soft and beginning to color, 8 to 10 minutes.

Add the asparagus to the pan and continue to cook until just tender, another 3 to 4 minutes.

Meanwhile, in a small bowl, beat the eggs with the cream and sprinkle with salt and pepper.

Reduce the heat to low and add the tarragon to the skillet. Pour the egg mixture over the vegetables, distributing evenly. Cook, undisturbed, until the eggs are just set and the edges of the frittata can be loosened from the sides of the pan with a spatula, 8 to 10 minutes.

Dot the top of the frittata with the goat cheese and lay the chives across in a random manner. Transfer the frittata to the oven and broil until the top just begins to bubble and brown, 1 to 2 minutes. Slide the frittata out of the pan and onto a serving plate; cut into wedges. Serve hot, warm, or at room temperature.

kale, spinach, and pecorino pizza slivers

CERTAIN FOODS HAVE THEIR MOMENT IN THE SUN; YOU KNOW, like those months when everyone was suddenly swooning over chia or smitten with açai. The kale phenomenon started quite a few years ago; one day, it was a toothsome leafy green languishing next to the collards and chard, and then suddenly it was being massaged with oil for salad, slow-cooked with sea salt for chips, and cold-pressed with ginger and green apples for juice. Kale was the "It" vegetable, the trendy brassica, the hipster green. But it wasn't until I had a pizza back home in Los Angeles at Stella Barra that I joined the legions of kale converts and became one of the annoying acolytes who swears life is just better with kale in the picture. The pizza that changed it all was topped with kale and spinach—the greens somehow being both tender and crisped at the same time. I was jealous not to have thought of this combination myself, eager to eat another slice before it all disappeared, and excited to try to make one similar. Kale, it seems, is truly one of the cool kids. *See photograph on page 135.*

2¾ cups bread flour	1 cup warm water	3–4 ounces baby spinach
¼ ounce active dry yeast (about 2½ teaspoons)	3–4 ounces kale (about ½ bunch), deribbed and leaves cut into 1" ribbons	2–3 tablespoons medium or coarse cornmeal
2 teaspoons sea salt		Wedge of pecorino cheese
¼ cup plus 3 tablespoons extra-virgin olive oil		

In a food processor, combine the flour, yeast, and salt. With the machine running, pour ¼ cup of the olive oil through the feed tube, then add the water in a slow, steady stream. Continue to process for 2 to 3 minutes (the dough should form a rough ball and ride around in the processor). The finished dough should be soft, slightly sticky, and elastic. If it seems a bit too dry, add a tablespoon or so of water; if it's too wet, add a tablespoon or so more flour.

Lay a piece of plastic wrap about 12" long on a clean work surface. Work the dough into an 8" × 5" rectangle on the plastic. Press your fingers into the top of the dough, making indentations all over as though it were a focaccia. With a long side facing you, fold the left third of the dough over (as you would a letter) and repeat the indentions. Fold the right third over and make the indentations again. Cover the folded dough with plastic wrap and let rise for 20 minutes.

Halve the dough, form each piece into a neat ball, wrap tightly in plastic wrap, and transfer to the freezer. The morning before you want to make pizza, transfer the dough to the refrigerator to thaw.

About an hour before you're ready to bake, put a pizza stone in the oven on the middle rack and preheat to 500°F. (If you don't have a pizza stone, oil a rimmed baking sheet and set aside.) Bring the dough to room temperature.

Meanwhile, in a large skillet, heat 2 tablespoons of the olive oil over high heat. Add the kale leaves and sauté, stirring frequently, until just beginning to wilt. Add the spinach and continue to cook, stirring constantly, until the greens are fully wilted, 2 to 3 minutes. Remove from the heat. Use a wooden spoon to press against the greens and squeeze out any extra liquid; discard into the sink (you don't want to make the pizza crust soggy).

Dust a pizza peel or the oiled baking sheet generously with cornmeal. Working with the dough in your hands (not flat on a work surface), gently begin to stretch the dough into a circular shape, pressing your fist up into the center of the dough and pulling at the edges with your other hand. With both hands, stretch the dough, being careful not to tear it. Working in a circular motion, pull the thicker edges of the dough outward, letting gravity help you. Continue to stretch the dough until it's relatively even in thickness (the edges will be thicker) and you have the size you want, 10" to 12" in diameter. When the dough is the size desired, carefully lay it on the peel or baking sheet.

Brush the crust with the remaining 1 tablespoon olive oil. Use a vegetable peeler to shave off slivers of pecorino and cover the top of the crust with a thin layer of the cheese. Drape the reserved greens evenly over the dough and layer more cheese on top. Carefully slide the pizza off the peel and onto your heated stone, or place the baking sheet in the oven. Bake the pizza until the crust is golden and the cheese is bubbling, 6 to 10 minutes. Serve immediately.

potato and thyme with taleggio pizzettes

I WROTE A BOOK ON HOMEMADE PIZZA. I MENTION this simply because once you come up with close to 100 or so ideas for all sorts of ingredients that can live happily together atop a pie, well, it's hard to pick a favorite. But the thing about this particular combination is that while it is a pizza—it has a crust with a cornmeal underbelly and blistered bubbles on top, no doubt—it really could be mistaken for something more. And it is one of my very favorites. The wonder of this pie is how the luscious, sort-of-stinky cheese mingles with the slender, barely there slices of potato, how the buttery leeks bounce off the smoky thyme. The joy here is that the flavors all conflate to become something elegant, something sophisticated, something so graceful that you might mistake it for a tart or a galette—something with a less-pedestrian name than pizza, with a title more dignified, more befitting its sumptuous character. Except the truth is, it's just a pizza. It just so happens to be a very good one.

2¾ cups bread flour

¼ ounce active dry yeast (about 2½ teaspoons)

2 teaspoons sea salt, plus more to taste

¼ cup plus 2 tablespoons extra-virgin olive oil, plus more for greasing the pan

1 cup warm water

2 large leeks, cleaned and thinly sliced

1 medium russet (baking) potato

Cornmeal

¼ pound Taleggio cheese

3–4 sprigs fresh thyme

Freshly grated Parmesan cheese

In a food processor, combine the flour, yeast, and salt. With the machine running, pour ¼ cup of the olive oil through the feed tube, then add the water in a slow, steady stream. Continue to process for 2 to 3 minutes (the dough should form a rough ball and ride around in the processor). The finished dough should be soft, slightly sticky, and elastic. If it seems a bit too dry, add a tablespoon or so of water; if it's too wet, add a tablespoon or so more flour.

Lay a piece of plastic wrap about 12" long on a clean work surface. Work the dough into an 8" × 5" rectangle on the plastic. Press your fingers into the top of dough all over, making indentations as though it were a focaccia. With a long side facing you, fold the left third of the dough over (as you would a letter) and repeat the indentions.

recipe continues

ALSO PICTURED: *Kale, Spinach, and Pecorino Pizza Slivers* (PAGE 132)

potato and thyme with taleggio pizzettes

Fold the right third over and make the indentations again. Cover the folded dough with plastic wrap and let rise for 20 minutes.

Cut the dough into 4 equal pieces, form each piece into a neat ball, wrap tightly in plastic wrap, and transfer to the freezer. The morning before you want to make pizza, transfer the dough to the refrigerator to thaw.

About an hour before you're ready to bake, preheat the oven to 500°F. Bring the dough to room temperature.

In a medium skillet, heat the remaining 2 tablespoons olive oil over medium-high heat until it shimmers. Add the leeks and sprinkle with salt. Reduce the heat to medium-low and cook, stirring frequently, until the leeks begin to soften, 10 to 12 minutes. Add a few tablespoons of water to the pan to keep them from browning and help them braise. Continue to cook, stirring occasionally, until the leeks meld together, another 8 to 10 minutes (they should almost have the consistency of jam).

Meanwhile, bring a medium saucepan of salted water to boil. Use a mandoline to very thinly slice the potato (you should almost be able to see through the slices). When the water boils, add the potato slices and cook for about 1 minute—the slices should be tender but not thoroughly cooked through. Drain the potatoes and set aside to cool.

Oil two rimmed baking sheets and dust them generously with cornmeal. Working with the dough in your hands (not flat on a work surface), gently begin to stretch each thawed ball into a circular shape, pressing your fist up into the center of the dough and pulling at the edges with your other hand. With both hands, stretch the dough, being careful not to tear it. Working in a circular motion, pull the thicker edges of the dough outward, letting gravity help you. Continue to stretch the dough until it's relatively even in thickness (the edges will be thicker) and you have the size you want, 6" to 8" in diameter. When the dough is the size desired, carefully lay it on a baking sheet. You should be able to fit two pizzettes on each sheet.

Using the back of a spoon or a rubber spatula, spread the leeks evenly on the prepared pizza crusts, being careful not to tear the dough. Dot the leeks with walnut-size pieces of Taleggio. Place the potato slices on the crust in a single layer with the slices partially overlapping. Sprinkle the pizzettes with the thyme and Parmesan to taste.

Transfer the baking sheets to the oven and bake until the crusts are nicely browned, the edges of the potatoes have colored and begun to curl, and the Taleggio is melted, 6 to 10 minutes.

chickpea fries with meyer lemon–scented aioli

I'M SLIGHTLY EMBARRASSED TO admit that while I had eaten at the world-famous Chez Panisse in Berkeley by the time I was 16, I did not know what a *panisse* was until a few years ago (potentially even more embarrassing: I didn't realize that the restaurant was named for a character in Marcel Pagnol's 1930s movie trilogy and not these delicious savory fries until even more recently). It's only marginally worrying that as a cook, I never bothered to investigate either of these things, but it honestly didn't occur to me to think about it until I was making chickpea fries alongside Mark Bittman for one of his *New York Times* videos. As the camera started to roll, Mark smiled knowingly and began, "Today we're making chickpea fries, also called *panisse* in France." What? These things we'd been working on for a week were called *panisse*? How late to the party was I? Pretty late, it turns out. If you like French fries, I'd wager you'll love these. And while I don't know the derivation of it, they're often cut into batons on the bias and served stacked in overlapping rows. Another thing I should probably bother to investigate.

½ cup extra-virgin olive oil, plus more for frying and the baking sheet

2 cups whole milk

2 cups water

1 tablespoon unsalted butter

1½ teaspoons sea salt, plus more for finishing

2¼ cups chickpea flour

1 garlic clove, finely minced

1 large egg yolk

Juice of 1 Meyer lemon, plus wedges for serving

Freshly ground black pepper

recipe continues

chickpea fries with meyer lemon–scented aioli

Generously oil a 13" × 9" rimmed baking sheet.

In a large saucepan, combine the milk, water, butter, and 1 teaspoon of the salt and bring to a boil. Reduce the heat and let the liquid come to barely a simmer, then gradually whisk in the chickpea flour, stirring constantly to avoid lumps. Continue whisking over medium heat until the mixture becomes very thick and holds its shape easily, 8 to 10 minutes.

Transfer the mixture to the prepared baking sheet, spreading it out to fill the pan evenly, and use an offset spatula to smooth the top. Cover the baking sheet with plastic wrap and chill in the fridge until fully set and firm, about 2 hours.

Meanwhile, using the flat side of a knife, mash the garlic with the remaining ½ teaspoon salt until it becomes a paste. Transfer to a small bowl and add the egg yolk. Whisk in half of the lemon juice and beat until foamy. Add ½ cup of the olive oil to the bowl and continue whisking until combined. Add the remaining lemon juice. Taste, add more salt if needed, and season with pepper. Refrigerate until it's time to serve.

Cut the chickpea mixture into batons about 1" wide and 3" long.

In a large skillet, heat ½" of olive oil until it shimmers. Working in batches so you don't crowd the pan, fry the *panisse* until golden brown on one side, 1 to 2 minutes. Turn and cook on the other side until nicely browned as well. Remove from the oil, drain on paper towels, and sprinkle generously with salt and pepper. Repeat until all the *panisse* are fried. Serve hot with the aioli and Meyer lemon wedges.

polenta cakes with shiitake mushrooms, roasted garlic, and thyme

MY FRIEND ANDI IS NOT A BORN COOK. SHE willingly admits that comfort in the kitchen is as elusive to her as a headstand during yoga class is to me. My belief is that anyone can cook if they have the inclination and interest, and while she might argue the point, she is living proof of this theory. About 10 years ago, Andi decided she wanted to make a pie for Thanksgiving. With the help of instructional emails beforehand and a few phone calls during the trickier parts on the day of baking, she made not one, but two pies—pumpkin and pecan. I didn't taste them, but I hear they were damn good.

Then, when my pizza cookbook came out, she decided to try her hand at that. (I know, a first-time cook who aims high—pie dough and pizza dough right out of the gate.) Her pizzas look wonderful (she's 3,000 miles away, so photos are my gauge) and her partner says they're perfect; I trust him. So Andi, a self-proclaimed kitchen novice and longtime vegetarian, is learning to cook at last. She claims she's ready to break out of her comfort zone and try something new, so this recipe is my challenge to her. She's been making my mushroom pizza for months now, which uses this same technique, so I know she's got this part down: shiitakes roasted with garlic and thyme to bring out their deepest, earthiest essence. All that's left is for her to try her hand at the polenta cakes. Having conquered two kinds of pies, I'm far from worried about her mastering a cake.

4 tablespoons extra-virgin olive oil	2 tablespoons unsalted butter	12–14 shiitake mushrooms, stems discarded and caps sliced
1 cup whole milk	½ cup freshly grated Parmesan cheese, plus more for garnish	3 garlic cloves, smashed
2 cups chicken stock, plus more as needed	Sea salt	Freshly ground black pepper
1 cup polenta (not instant)		4–5 sprigs fresh thyme

Coat a 13" × 9" rimmed baking sheet with 1 tablespoon of the olive oil.

In a large saucepan, combine the milk and 2 cups of the stock and bring to a boil. Slowly add the polenta to the pot, stirring constantly to avoid lumps. Once all the polenta has been added, reduce the heat to low and continue to stir almost constantly until the mixture is very thick and the grain is tender, about 30 minutes. If the polenta seems to absorb the liquid too quickly, add more stock, ½ cup at a time, and continue stirring.

When the polenta is very thick—it should pull away from the edges of the pan when stirred—add the butter and Parmesan, season with salt to taste, and stir to combine well.

Remove from the heat and pour the polenta onto the prepared baking sheet. Use an offset spatula to smooth the top. Cover with plastic wrap and chill until fully set and firm, about 1 hour.

Preheat the oven to 400°F.

In a medium lidded ovenproof saucepan or Dutch oven, heat 2 tablespoons of the olive oil over medium-high heat. Add the mushrooms and garlic and sauté until the mushrooms just begin to soften, about 3 minutes. Sprinkle with salt and pepper. Add the thyme, cover the pot, and transfer it to the oven to roast until the mushrooms are cooked through and the garlic is very soft and fragrant, 6 to 8 minutes. Remove from the oven and discard the thyme stems. Leave the oven on and line a baking sheet with parchment paper.

Use a 2" round cookie cutter to cut the cakes and transfer to the lined baking sheet. Bake until warmed through, 10 to 12 minutes. Remove from the oven and top each cake with a spoonful of the mushroom mixture and more Parmesan.

deep-fried artichokes and crispy lemons

THERE IS ONE REALLY IMPORTANT THING TO KNOW about fried artichokes, and it's a sad one: They make white wine taste terrible. I mean, really terrible. And it's not just fried artichokes, but any artichoke, even the long-stemmed, olive oil–marinated ones that no antipasti should be without. From what I gather, there's some organic acid or enzyme in the artichoke that doesn't play well with white wine, and Mother Nature evidently doesn't drink or doesn't care about those of us who do. Unfortunately, I can't offer a solution to this natural culinary disaster, but I have found a satisfactory workaround: When you make these flowerlike fried delicacies, have a Gimlet or another cocktail of your choosing. Problem avoided, if not solved. Another option, if you're still unconvinced and insist on having wine at the table, is this: Offer your guests two beverages, one to accompany the artichokes and one for everything else. With two drinks in hand, everyone might be twice as happy.

4 lemons	Olive oil or other vegetable oil, for deep-frying	Sea salt and freshly ground black pepper
8 globe artichokes		¼ cup all-purpose flour

Fill a large bowl with water. Halve and squeeze the juice of 2 lemons into the water, then drop in the rinds.

To prepare the artichokes, remove the tough outer leaves until you reach the tender pale yellow/green leaves. Cut off about 1" of the thorny top. Trim the stem of the artichoke by peeling off the outer green fiber, leaving about 2" of stem if possible. Slice the artichokes in half lengthwise, and scoop out the choke and discard (a melon baller works well for this). As you work, immediately put the artichokes in the lemon water to prevent oxidization.

Fill a deep pot with enough olive oil to just cover the artichokes and heat to 325°F (use a candy thermometer). Line a baking sheet with paper towels and set aside.

recipe continues

deep-fried artichokes and crispy lemons

While the oil is heating, dry the artichokes well with paper towels. Sprinkle generously with salt and pepper.

When the oil has reached 325°F, working in batches so as not to crowd the pot, add the artichokes and cook, turning occasionally with tongs, until a fork easily pierces the stem at its thickest point, 10 to 15 minutes. The outside should be deeply golden.

Remove the artichokes from the oil and drain well on the lined baking sheet. (You can prepare the artichokes up to this point and leave them out for a few hours until you're ready to finish.)

Slice the remaining 2 lemons into thin rounds and remove the seeds. While the oil is still hot, mix the flour with a sprinkle of salt and a grind of pepper and dust the sliced lemons with the flour mixture to barely coat. Drop the lemons into the hot oil and cook until just crisp, 1 to 2 minutes. Remove and let drain on the lined baking sheet next to the artichokes.

When ready to serve, reheat the oil to 365°F. Working again in batches, return the artichokes to the hot oil for a minute or so, just to crisp. Drain very well on paper towels and serve hot in the center of a small plate, with a sprinkle of sea salt and the fried lemons.

cassoulet cups with duck, sausage, and zucchini

WHEN I MET KEN, HE WAS A VERY PICKY EATER. On our second official date, I called and asked him if he wanted to go to dinner at Grange Hall. At the time, Grange Hall was a sweet little restaurant on Commerce Street in Greenwich Village, a cozy place that was serving farm-to-table fare long before anyone called it that. Resonant of the 1940s in décor, the room was always alight with a golden aura, the walls resplendent with murals depicting a folk story of a sea captain and his two estranged daughters (the twin townhouses across from the restaurant were said to have been built to house the warring women), and the music exactly as you'd hope, Ella or Billie or June Christy accompanied by the icy rattle of martini shakers.

When I asked Ken if he wanted to go, he said, "I don't know. What kind of food do they have?" *Really?* I thought. *It's taken all I have to make this call and you ask me this?* "Well, they have good food—you know, fish, chicken, the usual." "Okay, if they have chicken." An adventurous eater and cook even back then, I should have been deterred, but evidently love truly is blinding. We had a great time despite his hesitancy (I had the trout, he had the chicken), and I decided his food foibles were surmountable, which they have proven to be—almost completely. I mention all this because when I first decided I wanted to make cassoulet, I saw the deep consternation creep into Ken's lovely but telling eyes, the pull of his lips, the slightest, almost imperceptible shake of his head. "Do you not like cassoulet?" His response: "I don't know. What is it?" And with that, I knew he'd love it—and he does.

4 tablespoons extra-virgin olive oil, plus more as needed

1 pound sweet Italian sausages (about 4)

2 duck legs confit

2 garlic cloves, chopped

2 medium leeks, cleaned, trimmed, and thinly sliced

2 medium carrots, cut into ¼"-thick rounds

2 celery stalks, cut into ¼" pieces

2 medium zucchini, cut into ½" pieces

Sea salt and freshly ground black pepper

1 can (28 ounces) San Marzano tomatoes, drained (juice reserved for another use)

2 cans (15 ounces each) cannellini beans, rinsed and drained

About 3 cups chicken stock

3 sprigs fresh Italian parsley, chopped

4 sprigs fresh thyme, leaves picked, plus more for breadcrumbs (optional)

2 fresh bay leaves

Good pinch red chili flakes, or more to taste

2–3 cups homemade breadcrumbs

recipe continues

cassoulet cups with duck, sausage, and zucchini

In a large deep pot, heat 1 tablespoon of the olive oil over medium-high heat until it shimmers. Reduce the heat to medium, add the sausages, and cook, turning every few minutes, until nicely browned on all sides and cooked through, about 10 minutes. Remove the sausages from the pan and set aside.

In the same pot, add the duck legs, fat-side down, and cook over medium heat until they release easily from the pan and are deeply colored. Flip the legs and cook on the other side. When the second side is browned, use your tongs and hold the legs upright so the edges brown a bit too. Remove from the pan and let sit with the sausages.

If the pan seems dry, add another 1 tablespoon olive oil (you want about 2 tablespoons total fat in the pan). When the fat is hot, add the garlic and leeks and cook over medium heat, stirring frequently, until the vegetables begin to soften, about 6 minutes. Add the carrots, celery, and zucchini, sprinkle with salt and pepper, and cook until tender, another 8 to 10 minutes.

Meanwhile, tear the meat from the duck legs and discard the bones. Cut the sausages into ½" rounds.

Add the cut-up meat, the tomatoes (I just add them whole and break up with a wooden spoon in the pan, but feel free to roughly chop), beans, 2½ cups of the stock, the parsley, thyme, bay leaves, and chili flakes to the pan. Reduce the heat to medium-low, partially cover the pot, and let simmer for 1 hour, stirring every 15 minutes or so. After an hour, the mixture should have thickened and the beans should begin to break down a bit and create a creamy sauce. If the stew is still too thin, increase the heat to medium and cook for another 20 to 30 minutes; if it's too thick, add a bit more stock. Taste and adjust the salt, pepper, and chili flakes as needed. Fish out the bay leaves and discard.

Preheat the broiler.

Toss the breadcrumbs in a bowl with the remaining 2 tablespoons olive oil and some salt and pepper (I like to add a few sprigs' worth of thyme leaves too). Ladle the cassoulet into small broilerproof bowls. Sprinkle each serving with a nice coating of breadcrumbs and transfer to a baking sheet. Broil until the breadcrumbs are just golden, 2 to 3 minutes.

ALSO PICTURED: *Sautéed Sweet Onion and Chard Toast with Rustic Tomme* (PAGE 74), *left center*

shredded potato cakes with ramps

POTATOES, SHREDDED, PRESSED TOGETHER, AND fried in fat are pretty much my idea of bliss. Growing up, we called them hash browns and my mom served them for breakfast with fried eggs on special occasions. More often now they're dinner, needing nothing more than a salad to make the meal complete. Some people prefer potato cakes that rely on leftover mashed potatoes, but I like the rougher, more rustic texture of a shredded cake. With mashed cakes, you get that first crisp bite followed by a smooth inside that breaks down and collapses on your tongue, almost as if exuding a sigh of relief. With shredded cakes, the exterior, if cooked well, becomes a crunchy web enclosing a tender but still structured interior, a lace of starch, fat, salt, and any other seasoning you decide feels right.

Bits of leftover anything can go into a potato cake, so last spring, when a friend showed up bearing a bag of ramps she'd just picked that morning from a vacant lot near her Berkshire home, dinner was decided. Ramps, for those who don't live in a place where they grow wild, are the most seasonal and fleeting member of the onion family. Like a scallion's prettier cousin, these lithe alliums have pearly bulbs at one end with eggplant-colored waists and breezy wing-like tails that fan out into edible greens on the other. I hate to cut ramps, as they're so stunning when cooked whole and left in a tangle, but for this, you really want the heads to be tender without overcooking the stems or browning the leaves. If ramps aren't an option, a sweet onion will do the trick. Add some thyme, leftover sautéed mushrooms, bits of pancetta or bacon—really anything your heart desires.

3 medium russet (baking) potatoes, peeled

4–6 ramps, or less if that's all you have

6 tablespoons extra-virgin olive oil (or duck fat, if you're feeling decadent)

Sea salt and freshly ground black pepper

On the widest holes of a box grater, grate the potatoes. Working in batches, take a handful of the potatoes in a clean kitchen towel (you can use paper towels instead, but they tend to tear) and squeeze out as much liquid as you can. Put each batch of squeezed potatoes into a large bowl and set aside.

Separate the ramp leaves from the white stems and bulbs. Chop the bulbs and stems into bite-size pieces and cut the leaves into ribbons.

In a 12" nonstick skillet, heat 2 tablespoons of the olive oil over medium-high heat until it shimmers. Add the bulbs and stems, sprinkle with salt and pepper, and cook until tender, about 5 minutes. Add the leaves and continue to cook until they wilt, another 2 to 3 minutes.

Preheat the oven to 400°F. Line a baking sheet with parchment paper.

Season the shredded potatoes with salt and pepper. Add 2 tablespoons olive oil to the pan. Transfer the potatoes to the pan, tossing so the ramps are distributed evenly among the potatoes, and then use a spatula to press into a firm cake. Take the spatula around the edge of the pan and press the potatoes in a bit so you have a relatively firm patty. Reduce the heat to medium-low and let the cake cook undisturbed for about 15 minutes. Give the pan a shake to loosen the cake. Place a plate wider than the pan over the top of the pan and carefully invert the cake onto the plate. Add the remaining 2 tablespoons olive oil to the pan and slide the cake back into the pan with the browned side facing up. Continue to cook until a peek under the bottom of the cake shows it's browned, another 15 minutes.

Flip the cake out of the pan and onto the lined baking sheet. Transfer the cake to the oven and bake until the potatoes are tender all the way through, another 15 to 20 minutes. Serve hot or at room temperature.

shrimp-studded rice paper rolls and peanut dipping sauce

MY SISTER, ALI, AND HER HUSBAND, JEREMY, DID A very cool thing when they decided to get married. Instead of a traditional wedding, they threw an unassuming housewarming party, invited all their friends and family to their new loft, and then in the midst of it all, surprised the crowd by saying "I do" atop the spiral staircase in the middle of their living room. That was pretty nifty, but the really cool part is that Ali and Jeremy are friends with Charles Phan, the chef and owner of The Slanted Door, a renowned Vietnamese restaurant in San Francisco, who kindly offered to cater their unexpected nuptials. Charles's spring rolls are often the first thing I head for when I get off the plane in San Francisco and the last thing I grab before getting back on—they're that good. So besides Ali marrying Jeremy and the a cappella boy band who sang Drift Away following the ceremony, these spring rolls were the highlight of the party. And, while I've tried to make Charles's recipe many times since, they're never as good as his; so instead of feeling demoralized by what I can't perfectly replicate, I've devised a simpler version that doesn't aim so high. These are fresh, sweet, and wonderful in their own right, but full disclosure only seems fair: They're definitely different from the ones at The Slanted Door.

½ cup creamy unsweetened peanut butter

¼ cup water

2 tablespoons soy sauce

2 tablespoons honey

1½ tablespoons rice vinegar

1 teaspoon fresh lime juice

1 piece (1") fresh ginger, peeled

2 garlic cloves, peeled

¼–½ teaspoon red chili flakes

Pinch sea salt

4 ounces vermicelli (rice noodles)

2 tablespoons extra-virgin olive oil

18 medium shrimp, peeled and deveined

1 small head Boston or Bibb lettuce, leaves separated

Handful fresh mint or basil leaves, or a combination

1 carrot, julienned

1 Persian (mini) cucumber or ½ English cucumber, julienned

12 rice paper wrappers (8")

In a food processor, combine the peanut butter, water, soy sauce, honey, vinegar, lime juice, ginger, 1 garlic clove, chili flakes, and salt and process until very smooth. Taste to adjust the seasoning and add more water to thin a bit, if needed. Set the dipping sauce aside.

Bring a pot of salted water to boil and cook the vermicelli according to package directions. Drain in a colander and rinse with very cold water, then with very hot water, and then again with very cold water (this helps keep the noodles from sticking together). Set aside.

Mince the remaining garlic clove. In a medium skillet, heat the olive oil over medium-high heat until it shimmers. Add the minced garlic and cook for 30 seconds, stirring constantly. Reduce the heat to medium, add the shrimp, and sear on both sides until pink and cooked through. Remove from the heat. When cool enough to handle, slice each shrimp in half lengthwise and set aside.

Gather together the lettuce, noodles, mint, carrot, and cucumber and organize them so they're within easy reach. Fill a large bowl with very hot water. Soak and wring out two clean kitchen towels and lay one in the center of your work surface (this helps keep the rice papers from sticking). Working with one rice paper at a time, soak the paper in the hot water until tender and pliable, but not so long that it tears, 10 to 15 seconds.

Lay the rice paper on the towel. Line the bottom third of the paper with one lettuce leaf and top with about ¼ cup vermicelli. Add a couple of mint leaves and 2 or 3 pieces of carrot and cucumber on top of the noodles. Fold the bottom edge up over the vegetables and vermicelli and roll up tightly, just until the rice paper sticks to itself but you still have more rice paper to go. Lay three shrimp, cut-sides up, on the rice paper so they are touching the edge of the rolled portion. Now fold the right and left sides over the shrimp and rolled portion, and continue to roll up as tightly as possible until everything is completely enclosed and the sides are nicely tucked in. Move the roll to a plate and cover with the other damp towel to keep the rice paper from drying out. Repeat this process until you've used all the ingredients.

Cut the rolls into thirds on the bias and serve with the peanut dipping sauce.

last bites, small and sweet

I'm a selective sweets eater. I like a bite or two, but rarely need my own serving. So I've taken to making desserts that are meant to be shared, what I think of as intentionally communal sweets—an idea inspired by our friends Neil and Claude, who, at one of their dinner parties, placed a single platter of brownies and ice cream in the middle of the table, then casually dropped a spoon in front of each of us. It was relaxed yet sophisticated, the hosts making their own lives easier in the kitchen and all of us more comfortable at the table. None of the guests knew one another before that night, but suddenly we were scooping ice cream off the same plate and fighting over the last crumbs. Whether it's a platter of fruit, a smattering of crumble-topped ramekins, or a selection of cakes, ditching formality in favor of intimacy is refreshing. Try it.

an inspired platter of fruit and a piece of chocolate

NOT TOO LONG AGO, WE WERE INVITED TO A GROWN-UP dinner party. The kind where people you don't know very well sit around and talk about what they do for a living, what they thought of the new restaurant that opened up where the old restaurant used to be, and other topics that usually leave me wondering why we went in the first place. I tried to be a good guest by asking what I should bring—dessert, wine, anything at all—but the hostess very adamantly said no, she had it all taken care of.

After dinner, when the plates were cleared and the coffee was being poured, the hostess returned to the table with a bowl of small oranges and passed them around. How charming, I thought, this casual and refreshing reprieve between dinner and dessert. What a sweet, rustic touch, I noted, as I waited with bated breath for the homemade cookies, the froufrou torte from the French bakery down the street, or even a few bars of chocolate, the metallic wrappers torn back and passed around for all to share. Then whiskey came out, more coffee was proffered, and it dawned on me that this was it—a lone orange would punctuate this lackluster evening, the peel lying torn and pithy on the placemat in front of me.

Now, I'm not against fruit for dessert, don't misunderstand me, but for a dinner party, passing out oranges feels kind of meager, like you just couldn't be bothered. Sure, at home I'll happily peel an orange and share sections after a meal for something light and sweet, but guests deserve a bit more in my book. If you want to serve fruit (and by all means do), then spend a couple more minutes shopping and a few more slicing, and have fun playing with both succulent and surprising combinations. A fruit plate can dazzle if done with care and seasonality in mind. A chocolate bar is never a bad idea either.
See an additional photograph on page vi.

SUMMER FRUIT PLATE IDEAS	TROPICAL FRUIT PLATE IDEAS	FALL/WINTER FRUIT PLATE IDEAS
Stone fruits: cherries, apricots, peaches, plums, or nectarines	Pineapple	Figs
	Mango	Apples (tart and sweet)
Berries: raspberries, blueberries, blackberries, or strawberries	Papaya	Pears
	Kiwi	Red currants or pomegranate seeds
		Milk or dark chocolate bar, broken into bite-size pieces

Choose a selection of ripe, seasonal fruit and peel, pit, and slice or cut up the fruit as needed. Arrange on a plate or platter and serve with the chocolate. No one will want for more.

brown butter brownies

THERE ARE THINGS IN THIS LIFE THAT I CAN'T DO, NO matter how hard I try. Take, for instance, my love of music and lack of musical talent. From the moment I got my bubble-shaped white Panasonic tape recorder and my first cassette, *Get the Knack* (it was 1979, so totally cutting-edge), I pushed play and was smitten. Then Elvis Costello became my high-school heartthrob and the Sony Walkman my parents gave me twirled *Alison* so many times I'm surprised the tape wasn't wiped clean. I was a DJ in college, but it still wasn't enough. So I bought a used guitar and took lessons, to no avail. As Don McLean so aptly said, " . . . the music wouldn't play." I love to sing, and boy have I tried. But according to at least one source (Ken), I can't carry a tune, or at least not one that should be heard by others; so I'm reduced to belting it out with Sugarland alone in the car or crooning with Anita O'Day when no one else is home.

But here's the thing: I can brown butter. No, I may not be able to tell chord A from C, but I know how to judge when the milk solids are the exact shade of rusty brown to pull the pan off the stove. I can't sing on key (or tell one key from another), but I know when the bubbling, foamy fat is toasted just right so that these brownies have that perfect crackle-topped texture and moist, almost-fudgy-but-not-too-gooey interior. I am totally aware that making a great brownie is not the same as being a legendary jazz singer or a member of the Grand Ole Opry. I get that I'm never going to win that Grammy or sell out Madison Square Garden. But it makes me feel better to know that even if I can't sing or play, even if Ken never wants to hear my bluesy version of *Peaceful Easy Feeling* again (as he's told me repeatedly, he doesn't), then at least he will always want an encore when it comes to my brownies.

1¼ sticks (10 tablespoons) unsalted butter, cut into pieces, plus more for the pan

1¼ cups sugar

¾ cup unsweetened cocoa powder

½ teaspoon sea salt

¼ teaspoon baking powder

2 large eggs

1½ teaspoons vanilla extract

⅔ cup all-purpose flour

2 ounces dark or semisweet chocolate, roughly chopped

Flaky sea salt, for serving

recipe continues

ALSO PICTURED: *Lacy Oatmeal–Chocolate Chip Cookies* (PAGE 159)

brown butter brownies

Preheat the oven to 325°F. Line an 8" × 8" baking pan with two pieces of crisscrossed parchment paper, leaving enough overhang to pull the brownies out of the pan when baked. Butter the parchment paper well.

In a medium saucepan, melt the butter over medium heat, stirring pretty constantly with a heatproof spatula. Continue to cook for about 8 minutes, until it begins to brown (you want to see little brownish-reddish particles suspended in the melted butter). It should smell wonderful but will begin to color quickly at this point, so remove from the heat once you see the particles.

Stir the sugar into the saucepan and combine well. Then stir in the cocoa powder, salt, and baking powder until thoroughly incorporated. Let sit for a few minutes to cool.

Add the eggs to the pan one at a time, beating to incorporate into the mixture until it looks shiny and well blended. Add the vanilla and flour and stir until the flour is fully integrated, then give the mixture another minute of mixing to smooth out the batter. Add the chopped chocolate and stir until it's almost completely melted.

Spread the batter in the prepared pan, using a knife or offset spatula to smooth the top. Bake until a wooden pick or skewer inserted in the center comes out almost clean, about 25 minutes. Cool the brownies completely before using the parchment paper to lift them out of the pan.

Cut the brownies into small squares and serve on a large plate. Sprinkle with flaky sea salt and offer multiple forks and spoons and a couple pints of your favorite ice cream.

lacy oatmeal–chocolate chip cookies

I REMEMBER THE FIRST TIME I HAD AN OATMEAL-CHOCOLATE chip cookie. Our babysitter, Llewelyn—even her name was cool—brought over some cookies she'd made. This was the mid '70s, and as I remember, she was like a shorter version of Susan Dey in *The Partridge Family*, only more exotic. She had long brown hair that was parted right down the middle and fell in that loose, natural way that hair doesn't seem to fall anymore. She wore peasant skirts and had a guitar. She was studying modern dance and had written a children's book about a girl named Ivy. I wanted to be exactly like her. Especially after I tasted her cookies.

The day I tasted Llewelyn's oatmeal–chocolate chip cookies, I definitely knew what I had suspected all along—that the old-fashioned oatmeal cookie wasn't living up to its full potential. It was reticent, looking for that something to make it feel complete. Llewelyn had found what was missing—the chocolate chip. Her cookies were socially acceptable yet daring. They were part Ali McGraw and part Faye Dunaway. If I were a cookie, these were the cookies I imagined my 8-year-old self to be: good and well behaved on the outside but with a dark, brooding interior, a rebel dying to break out.

After years of tinkering and tweaking, the recipe I make now is a slightly more sophisticated relative of those cookies: crunchy and just a bit lacy, laden with chocolate chips and a halo of cocoa powder, full of oats but not overly earthy. Just as I remember them, these cookies are the girl next door on the back of a motorcycle, wholesome yet daring and rebellious at the same time. They're everything I'll never be, but damn they taste good. *See photograph on page 156.*

1 cup packed dark brown sugar

1 cup granulated sugar

2 sticks (½ pound) unsalted butter, at room temperature

2 large eggs

1 teaspoon vanilla extract

3 cups rolled oats

1 cup all-purpose flour

2 tablespoons unsweetened cocoa powder

1 teaspoon baking soda

1 teaspoon baking powder

¼ teaspoon sea salt

8 ounces good-quality chocolate, chopped into chunks, or chips

½ cup pecan pieces, toasted

¼ cup shredded coconut (sweetened or the natural stuff)

recipe continues

lacy oatmeal–chocolate chip cookies

Preheat the oven to 350°F. Line two baking sheets with parchment paper.

In a stand mixer fitted with the paddle attachment, cream the brown sugar, granulated sugar, and butter until the mixture is light and fluffy, about 5 minutes. Add the eggs and vanilla and beat, scraping down the sides of the bowl as needed, until fully combined.

In a large bowl, combine the oats, flour, cocoa powder, baking soda, baking powder, and salt and stir to combine. Add the dry mixture to the butter mixture and mix until just combined. Remove the bowl from the mixer and stir in the chocolate, pecans, and coconut.

Scoop tablespoon-size balls of dough onto the prepared baking sheets, leaving a good 2" between them. Bake until the cookies are crisp and golden brown, 12 to 14 minutes. Let the cookies cool on the pan for a few minutes, then transfer to a wire rack to cool.

> **Note:** *You can bake half of this recipe and freeze half if you like to make fresh cookies in a flash. Lay out a sheet of plastic wrap on the counter and transfer any unbaked dough to the center of the plastic. Use your hands to form the dough into a long log, then roll the plastic around it and twist tightly on the ends to freeze. The morning of the day you want to bake, transfer the dough to the fridge to thaw and then simply cut into pieces, form into balls, and bake when ready.*

apricot, berry, fig (or almost any kind of fruit) almond slices

I SPENT ABOUT A YEAR LIVING IN LONDON AFTER college. As it happens, I ended up making one of my very closest friends during that time. Our lives are woven together in many ways, but sadly, living in the same city again has never been one of them. Over the years, we've either met in foreign places to spend time together or traveled back and forth between New York and London for brief weekends. All this is a prelude to why this cake is here. Every time I go to visit Jackie, I'm drawn to the small café (now world-famous) by her flat in Islington called Ottolenghi. Since the first time I set foot in the milk-white shop, the windows piled high with pastel-colored meringues and buttery pastries, I have left with a fruit-topped slice of almond cake. The first time it was apricot, the next was pear, then peach, once fig.

Returning to New York after a short visit about 10 years ago, I took the bold step of emailing Yotam Ottolenghi to ask for the recipe, promising not to share it with a soul (this was prior to his cookbook fame and universal presence). He kindly wrote back (I was surprised but delighted) and said, "Well it's just a basic frangipane sponge topped with fruit." That was kind, but hardly enough for me to go on. Clearly no secret was going to be revealed, just a charming note to get me started on my quest to replicate the world's greatest cake. So I started playing around, and while we ate a lot of good almond cakes, they never came close to his. Then his first book came out and I was sure the mystery would be solved, but a quick glance at the index made my heart fall. He wasn't giving this one up.

Then one day I was browsing around his website and found a recipe for a fig cake using almond flour. Made in the round it looked more like a proper cake than the fruit squares I coveted from his shop, but the ingredients seemed promising. Unfortunately, I'll never know if this is exactly *the cake*, the one cut into stout little squares, the crumb moist and nutty and just my kind of sweet. By the time I get off the plane it's always gone, so I've never been able to compare the two, bite for bite, but this one works for me. I've simplified the aromatics, added almonds on top for a bit of crunch, and used all kinds of fruit imaginable, depending on the season and what I have that needs using up.

recipe continues

apricot, berry, fig (or almost any kind of fruit) almond slices

1¾ sticks (14 tablespoons) unsalted butter, at room temperature, plus more for the pan

1 cup sugar

3 large eggs, beaten

1 vanilla bean

1¾ cups almond flour

½ cup plus 3 tablespoons all-purpose flour

½ teaspoon sea salt

⅓ cup Greek yogurt

2–3 cups fruit of your choice, for topping: blueberries, sliced rhubarb and raspberries, quartered figs, sliced apricots, etc.

¼ cup sliced almonds, for topping (optional)

Preheat the oven to 400°F. Butter a 9" springform pan, line the bottom with a round of parchment, and butter the parchment.

In a stand mixer, cream together the butter and sugar until light and fluffy, about 5 minutes. With the mixer running on low speed, very slowly drizzle the eggs into the bowl. Stop the machine to scrape down the sides as needed, until all the eggs are fully incorporated.

Slice the vanilla bean down the center and peel open the sides as you would a book. Use a small paring knife to scrape out as much of the seeds as you can, and add to the bowl. Let the mixer run for a minute, until you can see little specks of vanilla evenly throughout the mixture.

In a medium bowl, combine the almond flour, all-purpose flour, and salt. With the mixer on low speed, add the dry ingredients and mix until barely combined. Remove the bowl from the mixer and fold in the yogurt. When the mixture is thoroughly combined and no streaks of yogurt are evident, transfer the batter to the prepared pan.

Use an offset spatula to smooth the top of the batter, then gently press just enough fruit into the top of the batter to cover the cake (you should still see the batter through the layer of fruit). Sprinkle with sliced almonds, if using, and transfer the pan to a baking sheet before placing in the oven.

Bake for 15 minutes, then reduce the heat to 340°F. Bake until the cake is just beginning to color on the edges and pull away from the sides of the pan and a wooden pick or skewer inserted in the center comes out clean, another 40 minutes. Let the cake cool completely in the pan before releasing from the springform sides.

lemon-lavender posset

POSSET . . . ISN'T THAT NAME ENOUGH TO MAKE YOU swoon, the word itself bringing to mind a funny little house somewhere in a mossy forest? Names can seduce, inspire, and help us define ourselves. And they can make the ordinary, extraordinary. Set before me an apple called Braeburn, a damson or mirabelle plum, a cheese with the wicked title of Dragon's Breath Blue or the magical Timberdoodle and I'm, well, tickled. This dessert, which is insanely easy by the way, sounds like something out of a Van Morrison song or a poem by John Donne—visions of green fields and weeping willows spring to mind. It's also just fun to say. Come on, try it: Have a posset with me.

2 cups heavy cream

¾ cup sugar

1–2 fresh lavender flowers

5 tablespoons fresh lemon, lime, or other citrus juice

Red currants or pomegranate seeds, for garnish (optional)

In a medium saucepan, combine the cream, sugar, and lavender and bring to a boil, stirring to dissolve the sugar. Once the mixture begins to bubble, reduce to a simmer and let cook for 3 minutes. Remove from the heat and stir in the lemon juice. Let sit for about 10 minutes for the flavors to meld.

Strain the mixture through a fine-mesh sieve and then pour into small glasses, jars, or cups. Let cool completely (if you don't, the top will wrinkle), then cover with plastic wrap and chill for at least 4 hours or until fully set. Serve topped with red currants or pomegranate seeds, if you like.

kahlúa–vanilla bean crème brûlée pots

I HAD A FRIEND IN COLLEGE WHO LIVED IN AN APARTMENT above the café where I worked. I was what is now referred to as a "barista," though back then we just called it the "girl who makes cappuccino." My friend worked as a waiter at the only really elegant restaurant in our small town, and he'd regularly stop in for a coffee before or after his shift.

He was darkly handsome and very exotic, with the unplaceable accent of someone who grew up in Iran, was of Armenian descent, and moved to California. We weren't close; in truth, we were just friendly acquaintances who talked when he came into the café and sometimes wandered over to the local dive bar together after we both got off work to sip what I then believed to be a fashionable late-night drink: Kahlúa and cream. A cloying combination, this rich, sweet concoction is almost more enjoyable to watch than to drink, the dark brown liqueur and the milky cream twisting and twirling like ballroom dancers in a glass of ice. With drinks in hand, we talked about novels and music: I lent him my copy of *Travesty* by John Hawkes; he gave me a mix tape of Billie Holiday and Marianne Faithful (lacking in delusions of artiness we were not).

Naturally, we fell out of touch and went our separate ways after college, but then one New Year's Eve in New York City, I looked up to see him working the line at the restaurant I'd been invited to (open kitchens being all the rage in New York in the 1990s). We said our hellos, said we should get together, and then it was midnight. A few years later, we passed one another on the street in the Village; we lived within blocks of each other, it seemed. Then, more years having passed, we ran into each other in a coffee shop, a silly full-circle trip back in time, and finally exchanged deeper hellos. Once again, we seem to be out of touch for now, but every time I reach for the Kahlúa and cream to make these custards, I can't help but think of him.

| 2 cups heavy cream | 1 vanilla bean | 3 tablespoons Kahlúa or other liqueur |
| 1/4 cup granulated sugar | 4 large egg yolks | Demerara sugar |

Preheat the oven to 300°F. Bring a kettle of water to boil. Place five 4-ounce ramekins in the bottom of a large roasting pan and set aside.

In a medium saucepan, combine the cream and granulated sugar. Use a paring knife to cut the vanilla bean down the middle lengthwise, then open the sides of the pod like a book, scrape out the seeds, and add them to the pan. Cook over medium heat until bubbles just begin to appear at the edges of the pan (do not boil). Remove from the heat and let sit.

In a large bowl, whisk the egg yolks and Kahlúa together. Gradually add the warm cream mixture, whisking constantly. Strain the mixture through a fine-mesh sieve set over a measuring cup. Pour the custard into the ramekins.

Place the roasting pan in the oven and pour the boiling water around the ramekins until it reaches halfway up the sides. Bake until the custard has set but is still wobbly in the center (it will set up as it cools), 20 to 25 minutes. Transfer to a rack to cool and then refrigerate for at least 4 hours.

To serve, sprinkle about a teaspoon or so of demerara sugar on each dish. Tilt the dishes gently from side to side to help spread the sugar. Use a torch to caramelize the tops evenly or set them under the broiler for a minute or two, keeping a close eye on them so they don't burn. Serve immediately.

whatever-you-fancy fruit crumble

I HAVE AN ABSURD COLLECTION OF RAMEKINS. I have rounds, ovals, and squares. I have deep and shallow. I have some in clusters of four, six, and eight. Someday, when I have the garage sale I keep threatening to have, I'm going to go through the cupboard where I keep this ridiculous array of ramekins and figure out which I should keep and which I can live without.

Though thinking about it now, I *do* sort of need them all. The reason, and this makes a lot of sense if you think about it, is that I never know exactly how many stalks of rhubarb will have pushed up, or how many raspberries will have ripened on the vines at the empty house next door. I can never be sure how many plums the kind woman who always tells me to "have a blessed day" at the farm stand will add to my bag, or how many peaches I'll rescue before the squirrels have their wily way. You see, without knowing how much fruit I'll have on hand, I can't be sure which ramekins I'll need, so I really do need them all. Especially the wide, low-sided ones because, come to think of it, Ken favors a relatively even balance of crumble topping to fruit. He claims the perfect crisp or crumble (and they really are the same thing, aren't they?) has equal parts fruit to pecan-oat-crunch in every bite, which makes sense. More sense than one person owning this many ramekins, for sure.

6 tablespoons cold butter, cut into small pieces, plus more for the ramekins

About 4 cups fruit, whatever you like: sliced peaches, plums, apricots, berries, rhubarb, etc. (or better, a mix)

2–3 tablespoons granulated sugar (depending on how sweet your fruit is)

Grated zest of 1 orange or lemon, plus 1 tablespoon juice

¾ cup packed light or dark brown sugar

½ cup all-purpose flour

½ teaspoon ground cinnamon, or to taste

Good pinch sea salt

½ cup rolled oats

½ cup pecans

Preheat the oven to 375°F. Butter small ramekins or one large gratin dish and transfer to a baking sheet.

In a large bowl, toss the fruit with the granulated sugar and orange or lemon zest and juice and spread it out evenly in the ramekins or gratin dish.

In a food processor, combine the butter, brown sugar, flour, cinnamon, and salt and pulse until it looks like small peas and just begins to clump together, 20 to 30 seconds. Add the oats and pecans and pulse just a few times to combine (they shouldn't get too ground up).

Crumble the topping over the fruit and bake until golden and beginning to brown, 20 to 30 minutes for small ramekins and 45 to 50 minutes for a larger gratin dish.

classic crostata,
one large or a few small

IT HAPPENS EVERY YEAR. WINTER BECOMES THE GUEST that doesn't know it's time to leave, the season that overstays its welcome. Come April, the snow loses its novelty and I'm bored by the cold company, the incessant battleship-colored skies. But still it lingers, until even the trees begin to irritate me, so bare and spindly, some bone white, some ashen gray. Then one day a slight green shadow is there. Not buds yet, but a hue, tone, a tint to the air around them that says spring is coming. And then it does, quite quickly; like a film shown on fast forward, the trees flower and fruit appears and the long white wait is over.

One day the light changes from pale to gold and the fruit trees begin to compete with the birds to show who is more alive. And this is when I know that soon, I am going to make a pie. Well, not a pie so much as a tart, a galette—okay, let's agree to call it a crostata. The dessert that does what a good fruit dessert should do: showcase the fruit while letting the crust—perfectly flaky, delicate, and barely there—hold it all together without drawing too much attention to itself. This is the dessert that takes minutes (honestly) to make, yet looks like a painting. When I make this dessert, I am transported to the countryside somewhere: Italy probably; France maybe; New England possibly; okay, California. It's warm out, the sun is rich, and this dessert is summer on a crust.

1¼ cups all-purpose flour, plus more as needed

1 stick (8 tablespoons) very cold unsalted butter

1 teaspoon sea salt

¼–⅓ cup ice water

3 firm, tart apples or fruit of your choice

Good squeeze fresh lemon juice

4 tablespoons sugar, plus more for sprinkling

2 tablespoons all-purpose flour

In a food processor, combine the flour, butter, and salt. Process the mixture until it resembles small peas, 10 to 12 pulses. Transfer the dough to a large bowl and add ¼ cup of the water. Use your hands to integrate the water into the dough, adding a bit more if needed to bring it together. I often find I need to add another 2 tablespoons to get it all combined. Don't be scared of the dough, but don't overwork it either—it won't be homogenous: You should see chips of butter in the dough. If you're making one large crostata, form the dough into a flat disk, wrap it in plastic wrap, and refrigerate for 1 hour or up to 2 days. If you want to make 4 smaller crostatas, separate the dough into 4 pieces and form each into a small, flat disk before wrapping and refrigerating.

recipe continues

classic crostata, one large or a few small

While the dough chills, peel the apples and slice them very thinly (I use a mandoline here to make it easier and more consistent). If you're using other fruit, thinly slice as well—peaches and plums both work well. You can also add a handful of berries to the mix.

Toss the apples in a large bowl with the lemon juice—use more or less depending on your own taste, but know that this also helps keep the apples from browning—along with 2 tablespoons of the sugar.

Once the dough is well chilled, unwrap it and place it on a clean, lightly floured work surface. Use your rolling pin to hit the dough a few times to flatten and make it a bit easier to roll out. If you're making one large crostata, roll the dough into a large round about ⅛" thick (the edges will be scraggly, which is fine), then drape the dough over your rolling pin and transfer it to a parchment-lined baking sheet. If you're making multiple smaller crostatas, do the same for each of the 4 pieces of dough but use two baking sheets.

Preheat the oven to 375°F.

Meanwhile, in a small bowl, combine the flour and the remaining 2 tablespoons sugar. Either spread the mixture in the center of the large crostata, leaving about a 2" border, or spread it equally among the 4 smaller crostatas, leaving about a 1" border. Top the sugar-flour mixture with the fruit, using more or less depending on how much fruit you like, and then fold the edges of the dough in over the fruit in pleats, so that you have a border of dough with the majority of the fruit exposed in the center of the crostata. Chill the crostatas for 15 to 20 minutes while the oven heats.

Just before baking, brush the edges of the dough with water, sprinkle with more sugar, and transfer to the oven. Bake until the crust is golden brown and the fruit is bubbling, 20 to 25 minutes.

chocolate whiskey cakes with boozy vanilla cream

THERE ARE TWO KINDS OF PEOPLE IN THIS WORLD: those who love chocolate desserts and those who love fruit desserts. I suppose there are also those who like all desserts and then those who don't really go in for sweets at all, but generally speaking people seem to fall into one of the two camps. So here's a word of advice: If you're dating someone, it's worth finding out which camp they're in early on. I was not given this advice and as a result, I am a fruit-dessert person married to a chocolate-dessert person, and let me tell you—it causes no end of trouble.

Whenever we are having friends over and I want to bake, my instinct is to make a lemon tart, a raspberry-plum crumble, a rhubarb-apple crisp, maybe a peach crostata. Being the sort of spouse who listens to her partner and seeks to find compromise whenever possible, I usually toss out my ideas and then ask Ken what he would like. And this is where the problems begin; his answer to this question is, without fail, "Something chocolate." If I push back ever so gently and say, "But what about a pie?" his response is certain to be along these lines: "Sure, a chocolate cream pie, you mean?" And if I do get my way and lament not being able to find the fruit I want for a particular dessert, this is his pithy retort: "Well you know, chocolate is never out of season."

Is this proclivity for chocolate over fruit nature or nurture? I'm not sure, but Ken's mom did make a delicious double-chocolate Bundt cake that he ate regularly throughout his childhood and well into adulthood. It was made from a Duncan Hines mix, to which she added a box of chocolate Jell-O pudding, a bag of chocolate chips, and sour cream. This is very tough to compete with. So I don't try. Instead, I make these rich, barely boozy chocolate cakes topped with a spiked whipped cream. And here's the kicker: I finish each one with a handful of raspberries. Some might say that's passive-aggressive of me, but I think of it as pure compromise. He gets his chocolate, I get my fruit, and marital bliss is maintained.

recipe continues

chocolate whiskey cakes with boozy vanilla cream

2 sticks (½ pound) unsalted butter, plus more for the pan

1 cup unsweetened cocoa powder, plus more for dusting

1½ cups strong brewed coffee

½ cup whiskey, plus a splash for the whipped cream

2 cups granulated sugar

2 cups all-purpose flour

1¼ teaspoons baking soda

½ teaspoon salt

2 large eggs

2 teaspoons vanilla extract

1 cup cold heavy cream

1 tablespoon powdered sugar, or more to taste

1 cup raspberries

Preheat the oven to 325°F. Butter a 6-mold mini-Bundt pan well, then dust with cocoa powder (the cocoa powder means you won't get streaks of flour on your cakes) to coat well. Tap out any excess.

In a medium saucepan, combine the coffee, whiskey, butter, and cocoa powder. Whisk constantly over medium heat until the butter is melted. Remove from the heat and pour in the granulated sugar, whisking until it's fully dissolved. Let cool for about 5 minutes.

Meanwhile, in a small bowl, combine the flour, baking soda, and salt. In a large bowl, mix together the eggs and 1 teaspoon of the vanilla.

Add the chocolate mixture to the eggs and stir to combine. Add the dry ingredients and stir until just combined but no traces of flour are visible. The batter will be relatively thin in consistency.

Pour the batter into the prepared molds. Bake until a wooden pick or skewer inserted in the center comes out clean, 25 to 30 minutes. Let the cakes cool until they pull away from the edges of the pan, about 30 minutes. Turn out onto a rack and let cool completely.

Before serving, in a stand mixer (you can also use a hand mixer or even a whisk), whip the cream on medium speed until soft peaks begin to form. Add the powdered sugar, remaining 1 teaspoon vanilla, and a splash of whiskey (you can also use Grand Marnier, Cointreau, Kahlúa, or any liqueur or liquor you like), and continue to whip until the cream holds stiff peaks, being careful not to overwhip.

Serve the cakes topped with the cream and a sprinkling of raspberries.

Fathers day Brunch

graze -

pg ~~78~~ -96 - Rst brussel sprouts w/ pancetta
                    + maple pecans

73 - Shishito peppers

69 - pear crisps - w/ belsamic
                        glaze.

38 - Lemon Hummus

10 - figs + Serrano ham

81 - parsnip

87 - parmesan crisps

37 - Spiced carrots

1   Shrimp

Baked brie

bread - day ahead

Shrimp 1 day ahead.

bacon

Fruit crumble . 168

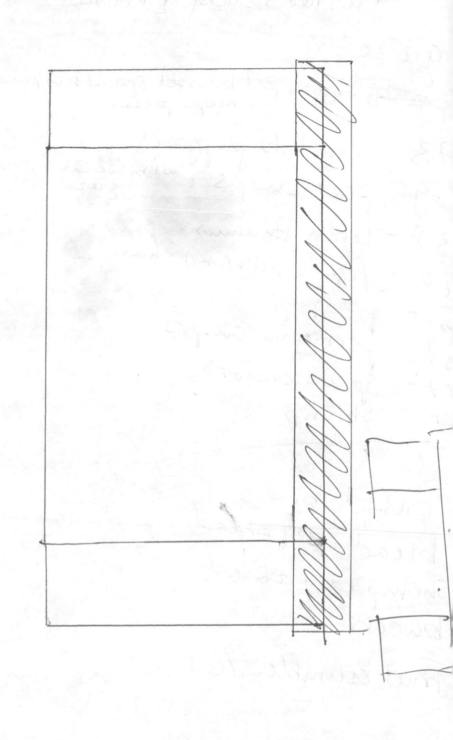

eiffel tower–inspired coconut macaroons

THERE ARE SCENTS THAT SEND ME SPINNING, AROMAS that must be so deeply embedded in my memory that with barely a whiff, I can experience déjà vu so vivid it throws me off balance. The moist, minty smell of eucalyptus hurtles me home to California with such suddenness that I can almost hear the rustle of those bluey-green leaves, the hot Santa Ana winds blowing mischievously through the branches. Stepping into an elevator with a woman wearing Diorissimo, the perfume my mom has worn for as long as I can remember, and my brain is addled, certain that somehow she's there next to me. And then there's coconut, that tropical, milky, sweet smell that swirls me off to a sandy beach faster than anything I can imagine. This warm exotic aroma competes with vanilla for the most alluring of food fragrances, and no other dessert offers up more pure coconut-ness than the macaroon.

Different from *macarons*, the sophisticated French confection made of meringue and almond flour, coconut macaroons require just five ingredients and can be made in mere minutes. They are usually formed into rounds and then baked, like tropical snowballs, just a touch of gold on the edges. But this approach is more festive by far, a whimsical twist on tradition: Mold the coconut mix into miniature pyramids and the edges will turn a delicious shade of bronze, as though tanned under a sweltering island sun, while the interior stays tender and chewy.

3 cups unsweetened coconut flakes

1 cup sugar

Pinch salt

3 large egg whites

1 teaspoon vanilla extract

Preheat the oven to 350°F. Line a baking sheet with parchment paper.

In a medium bowl, combine the coconut, sugar, and salt. Add the egg whites and vanilla and mix until you have a relatively cohesive blend.

Wet your hands and scoop out a rounded tablespoon of the mixture into the palm of one hand. Use your other hand to press in on both sides, bringing the macaroon to a point. Continue pressing with your thumb and forefinger on both sides until you have an even shape.

Place the pyramids on the prepared baking sheet and bake until golden at the edges, about 12 minutes. Let set on the baking sheet for a couple of minutes before transferring to a rack to cool completely.

the grazing breakfast (for guests or not)

Years ago, friends invited us up to their country house for the weekend. Being early risers, we awoke in the morning to a silent house, so we pattered into the kitchen hoping to quietly make some coffee and sit on the deck until everyone else stirred. To our surprise, we found breakfast spread across the old workbench that had been reclaimed as a center island. There was homemade fruit bread, a plate of muffins, a jar of granola, bowls of yogurt and fruit, a hot pot of coffee, and a pitcher of fresh juice. It seemed our intrepid hosts had snuck out, laid their premade goodies on the counter, and returned to snooze, allowing everyone to enjoy the morning on their own schedule. It was simple, smart, and delightful—and it's why there are so few things in this chapter, because the perfect grazing breakfast requires only some basics you can buy (the yogurt and fruit) or make ahead (the granola and baked goods). The goal is really for everyone to ease into the day as they see fit. That means the hosts too.

the brazilian breakfast

SOMETIMES YOU HAVE TO REALLY WORK TO GET LOST ON THIS planet. A flight from Rio de Janeiro to Salvador de Bahia, a ferry to the island of Morro de São Paulo, a small motorboat to Valença, and then a tractor through tangled and swampy mangroves to a secluded spot on the wisp of the island called Boipeba—this is how Jackie and I found ourselves in delightfully plain stucco-walled, thatch-roofed bungalows on a seemingly undiscovered beach, hammocks strung up outside each front door like woven welcome signs swaying gently in rhythm with the tide. Our host at this quiet *pousada* was a bearded, feral-looking man who we never saw wearing anything other than an orange bathing suit, his smooth skin burnished copper, the color of a new penny.

On our first morning, we woke to see wild horses cantering down the sand and young boys, slim as gazelles, practicing *capoeira*, the beautiful Brazilian martial art that's more acrobatic dance than aggressive fight, and we knew this was a spot worth the trouble it took to get there. Breakfast, a smattering of fruit in all shades of a sunset, was further proof. The mangoes we had seen growing wild on the trip over were the centerpiece, surrounded by sliced papaya, banana, guava, passion fruit, and even avocado, which was drizzled lightly with honey. There was a bowl of something creamy—a local yogurt, we assumed—a dish of muesli, half a baguette, a couple pots of different jams, and a tender, slightly salty fresh cheese.

Accompanied by a pot of strong coffee and a pitcher of thick cream, this was like no breakfast we'd stumbled upon so far. I still harken back to this oddly sophisticated but simple spread when I have guests; an inspired plate of fruit, some good bread, butter, and cheese or jam—what more could you want? Well, perhaps the hammock and the nearly deserted island, but that part's not so easy.

Fruit that works together (think seasonally and thematically): peaches, plums, apricots, and berries; or mangoes, papaya, bananas, star fruit, pineapple, and kiwi

Greek yogurt

My Granola (page 181)

Baguette or other good-quality bread

Butter and at least 2 kinds of jam (I like apricot or peach and a berry)

Cheese (something soft like Vermont Creamery's Cremont or a Brie)

Meat (think ham, salami, or any charcuterie) or smoked fish (optional)

Peel, cut, or slice the fruit as needed and spread it out on a platter. Put out a dish of yogurt and a jar of granola. If you like, toast the bread; though if it's really fresh, don't bother. Put out a plate of butter and jars of jam. Set out the cheese and, if you like, also put out a plate of thinly sliced meat or smoked salmon, haddock, or mackerel. Make coffee with hot milk on the side, offer up tea, and call it a day.

my granola

I CAN BE DISLOYAL; JUST ASK BREAKFAST. FOR YEARS I SKIPPED
it; I drank coffee or tea instead. Or I'd go through phases: croissants for a while, dry wheat toast, fruit and yogurt, bagels with cream cheese and tomato—I've had dalliances with them all. Each marks a certain time in my life, but I stuck with none of them. Until granola came along. Of course I'd eaten granola; during a stint in college we were even exclusive for a while, but then I moved on. I'd tasted a few kinds over the years that I liked very much, and when that happened I'd make a mental note of what made them stand out from all the others, you know, the ones languishing in bins at the health food store or on the shelves at the market. But breakfast wasn't my meal, so I didn't take any of it too seriously.

Then one day a friend said she was making her own granola and offered to send me some recipes she'd found. I still can't explain it, but looking at those recipes (all very different but representative of the same idea), I felt like there was a relationship out there I'd been missing without even realizing it. Breakfast was an entire meal I had written off without so much as a second thought, and granola was just part and parcel of that neglect. I guess this is how all love stories go: A friend introduces you and then nature takes its course. At least that's how it was for me. From the recipes she gave me, I pulled out bits and pieces from each that I liked. I began to play with different combinations of grains and nuts and various sweeteners. That's all granola is, really—a bunch of good stuff mixed up and toasted. It wasn't immediate, but it developed over time.

After a couple years of tweaking, I came up with a mix that's a perfect match for me. Until this granola, I admit, I treated breakfast as a second-rate meal, an on-again-off-again affair: one to fumble through sleepily en route to a more thoughtful lunch and then later a fully orchestrated and appreciated dinner. I was so fickle and unfair. But I've changed, really. Now granola and I spend most mornings together, even on the weekends. It's gotten serious.

recipe continues

my granola

6 tablespoons unsalted butter

⅓ cup packed light or dark brown sugar, or to taste

⅓ cup honey, or to taste

¼ cup maple syrup, or to taste

2 tablespoons vanilla extract

1 teaspoon sea salt

6 cups rolled oats

3 cups brown rice crisps

3 cups puffed wheat

1 cup coarsely ground almonds

1 cup coarsely ground pecans

1 cup coarsely ground walnuts

½ cup sliced almonds

½ cup unsweetened shredded coconut

1 tablespoon ground cinnamon

Preheat the oven to 325°F.

In a saucepan, combine the butter, brown sugar, honey, and maple syrup and heat over medium-low heat until the butter is melted. Add the vanilla and salt and stir well to combine.

In a really large bowl, mix together all the dry ingredients, including the cinnamon. Slowly pour the butter mixture into the dry ingredients, mixing to coat the oats, rice, and nuts as evenly as possible. Don't rush this: It will take a few minutes to thoroughly combine the butter with the dry ingredients.

Spread the mixture evenly on two baking sheets and bake for 15 minutes. Gently turn the granola using a spatula and bake for another 15 minutes, then turn again. The granola is done when it's a nice nutty brown color throughout, 30 to 40 minutes total. Remove the granola from the oven and let cool completely on the baking sheets. It will crisp up as it cools.

Store in an airtight container for up to 1 month or more. Serve with fresh fruit and yogurt or milk, or sprinkle over ice cream.

cherry-almond (or whatever) cream scones

SCONES SHOULD BE LIGHT AND NOT TOO SWEET; THEY should have a slight crunch followed by a tender crumb, and they should be rich but never heavy. Scones should not have the slightest metallic taste, the one that comes from using too much baking powder. They should not be dense and they should not be too big. To make really good scones, you need to handle the dough with confidence but without overworking the gluten. These scones are all that, and the beauty of this recipe is that you can play with the flavorings with wild abandon as long as you keep the quantities the same. Switch out the cherries for dried apricots and you have an apricot-almond scone. Fancy a lemon-blueberry scone and all you have to do is swap in ¾ cup frozen blueberries (frozen means they won't squish when you shape the dough) for the cherries, skip the sliced almonds and add the zest of a lemon, maybe a squeeze of the juice, and use vanilla extract instead of almond. As long as you don't overload them, these scones can handle an abundance of culinary creativity, and they can be done and dusted in under 30 minutes. One note: Do not try to use half-and-half or milk instead of the cream, or the scones will be rubbery; the mottled crust and tender crumb are dependent on the fat.

2 cups all-purpose flour

¼ cup granulated sugar

2 teaspoons baking powder

½ teaspoon sea salt

¾ cup chopped dried cherries or other fruit

¼ cup sliced almonds

1¼–1½ cups heavy cream, plus more for brushing

½ teaspoon almond extract

2 tablespoons demerara sugar

Preheat the oven to 425°F. Line a baking sheet with parchment paper.

In a large bowl, combine the flour, granulated sugar, baking powder, and salt. Add the cherries and almonds and stir to combine. Add 1¼ cups of the cream and the almond extract and stir just until a dough forms (depending on the weather, you may need to add up to another ¼ cup of cream to get all the flour fully incorporated). The dough should be just a bit sticky but not so much that you can't handle it easily.

Turn the dough out onto a lightly floured surface and knead it once or twice, until it holds together. Form the dough into an 8" round about 1" thick. Use a pastry cutter or long knife to slice the dough into 8 equal wedges.

Transfer the wedges to the prepared baking sheet. Brush the scones lightly with a bit more cream and sprinkle with the demerara sugar.

Bake until golden brown, about 18 minutes. Transfer to a rack to cool.

carolyn's banana bread, circa 1971

MY MOM HAS BEEN MAKING THIS RECIPE SINCE I WAS born—well, almost. It's from an old *Sunset* magazine paperback cookbook, slim as a matchbook and studded throughout with quirky line drawings of food rather than color photographs. But it's everything you want in banana bread: It rises high in the pan with a craggy fault line down the center, it's moist in the middle, and most importantly, it tastes like bananas. The original recipe called for margarine (it was 1971, remember), but butter is what you want. My mom started reducing the sugar from 1 cup to ¾ cup and adding shredded coconut years ago—that's the secret ingredient. It makes this bread more complex and slightly earthy (there's whole wheat flour in there, too), with a just a suggestion of something exotic because of how the bananas, coconut, and walnuts meld together. If you're having guests and want to be hands-off in the kitchen, make this loaf ahead—it freezes beautifully.

1 stick (8 tablespoons) unsalted butter, plus more for the pan

¾ cup sugar

2 medium very ripe bananas, well mashed (about 1 generous cup)

2 large eggs, beaten

1 cup all-purpose flour

1 cup whole wheat flour

1 teaspoon baking soda

½ teaspoon sea salt

⅓ cup hot water

½ cup chopped walnuts

¼ cup shredded coconut (sweetened is my preference, but natural is fine)

Preheat the oven to 325°F. Butter a 9" × 5" loaf pan.

In a small saucepan, melt the butter over medium-low heat. Pour into a large bowl, add the sugar, and use a wooden spoon or spatula to mix well. Add the mashed bananas and eggs and continue mixing until well combined.

In a medium bowl, combine the all-purpose flour, whole wheat flour, baking soda, and salt. Add the dry ingredients to the banana mixture alternately with the hot water in three additions.

When the batter is fully combined, stir in the nuts and coconut. Pour the batter into the prepared loaf pan and bake until a wooden pick or skewer inserted in the center comes out clean, 45 to 50 minutes. Let the bread cool in the pan until it releases from the sides, about 15 minutes, then transfer to a wire rack.

a few signature sips

As a wine drinker, I can be counted on to reach for a dry Burgundy over a dirty martini any day, but every now and then, when the sun's just dipping down on a summer evening, or the fire is shooting sparks on a cold night, it's nice to switch it up. We have a small collection of cocktails reserved for weekend evenings when we feel like something special, or when we have friends over and want to start the visit with a celebratory tipple. These are drinks served on the small size, aperitifs fit for a low-slung coupe or simple rustic water glass; they're designed to whet the palate and stir the senses, not dull them.

negroni fizz

I'M A SUCKER FOR A COOL HOTEL BAR. WALK ME INTO AN ELEGANT oak-paneled room with soaring ceilings, velvet banquettes, and copper-coated light fixtures all aglow, and my heart warms. Show me to the unassuming corner of a dimly lit lobby, a cozy alcove concealing a worn mahogany bar tattooed with drink rings, red leather–backed stools, and a blinking neon sign, and I'm giddy. There's something inherently romantic about these places. Unlike airport bars—which have their own tacky and fluorescently lit charm—hotel bars aren't intentionally bland stopovers to keep you sated before the adventure begins, but places you sink into once you've reached your final destination, spots to help you adapt and savor the accomplishment of having arrived.

When I find myself in a hotel bar, I'm often compelled to skip my usual glass of wine in a favor of a grown-up drink, something that makes me feel like I know much more about the world than I do: A Negroni, the most succulent and sexy of drinks, is my aperitif of choice. This Italian concoction has a way of being both exotic and familiar at the same time, not unlike a good bartender, one you've just met who still treats you like a regular. Sometimes, when I'm home and want to pretend I'm somewhere new and novel, somewhere that whispers of adventures yet to come, I make this bubbly version of a Negroni: Old Tom–style gin, if you've got it on hand, is slightly sweeter than London dry and gives this adaption a soothing honeyed-bitter balance, and the splash of fizz adds a glint of lightness. It's a bit less cloying and softer than the traditional mix, but it's transporting nonetheless. Just ask Ken, who says that with one of these in hand, I'm prone to babbling on about all the places we should go; two drinks in, and he has to stop me from pricing tickets to Patagonia, Havana, perhaps Tangiers, I hear Prague is nice this time of year . . .

4 ounces Ransom gin (or other Old Tom–style gin)	4 ounces Campari	Seltzer, for topping
	3 ounces dry white vermouth	Orange peel, for garnish

In an ice-filled glass or shaker, combine the gin, Campari, and vermouth and mix or shake to chill. Strain into 4 coupes and top with a splash of seltzer. Garnish with an orange peel.

blood orange blizzard

THIS DRINK HAS A RIDICULOUS NAME, THE KIND YOU MIGHT expect to find on the menu at a bar serving slushy blue drinks with curly straws. But before you dismiss it part and parcel, let me explain. Ken loves a gin Gimlet, especially the ones I make with my parents' Mexican limes. But on one particular Saturday in the middle of January, I found myself with two fresh blood oranges left over from a job the day before and couldn't resist trying something new. Ken winced a bit as I poured his favorite dry gin into the rosy mix, grimaced ever so slightly as I skipped the Rose's lime juice in favor of St-Germain liqueur (that wonderfully fragrant elixir made from elderflowers that comes in a beveled bottle worthy of expensive perfume). He stood by looking worried as I shook and stirred, but it took no more than a sip before he was convinced. And while all this boozy drama was unfolding in our kitchen, 30 inches of snow was blanketing New York City, a blizzard of historic proportions, the weather conspiring to give a rather sophisticated cocktail a very silly name.

4 ounces No. 3 London Dry Gin or other dry gin

4 ounces fresh blood orange juice

1½ ounces St-Germain liqueur

Blood orange slices, for garnish

In an ice-filled glass or shaker, combine the gin, blood orange juice, and St-Germain and mix or shake to chill. Strain into 4 chilled stemmed glasses. Garnish with slices of blood orange.

the weekender

HERE'S THE FUN THING ABOUT THIS DRINK: IT'S ADAPTABLE for those who prefer a sweeter libation or for those who are partial to a touch of bitterness. I think of it as the Little Black Dress of drinks; you can make it sweeter or edgier depending on your mood. In the summer, Ken tends to drink gin and tonics with lime as his aperitif, while every now and then I like a Campari and soda with a slice of orange.

One July evening, in an effort to simplify the predinner patio drink regimen, I decided to come up with something new, something that didn't require completely different ingredients and multiple kinds of citrus. Keeping Ken's predilection for gin in mind, I started there for both of us. Then I added Pimm's, that classic English liqueur, to his glass and Campari to mine (he's not a fan of the bitter nectar like I am). Topping them both with a generous splash of blood orange–flavored Pellegrino (you can use another flavor, of course), we had devised two cocktails out of one, a feat he immediately coined, "The Weekender," a pretty red drink perfect for warm evenings, whether your taste runs toward the English or the Italian.

6 ounces No. 3 London Dry Gin or other dry gin

3 ounces Pimm's No. 1 or Campari, depending on your taste

Blood orange San Pellegrino, for topping

Orange slices, for garnish

In an ice-filled glass or shaker, combine the gin and Pimm's or Campari and mix or shake to chill. Strain into 4 ice-filled martini or coupe glasses and top with the Pellegrino. Garnish with orange slices.

the franken-mojito

IN OUR HOUSE, DRINKS ARE USUALLY INVENTED out of necessity. I don't mean someone says, "I really need a drink," though that does happen with remarkable frequency. I mean because I often don't have whatever ingredients I need to make said drink, so I have to improvise; if my madcap substitutions actually work, then we have a new cocktail in our repertoire. In this particular case, a new drink came into being because my mint plant had a bad week. I'd left it out in the sun during a few brutally hot days and many of its tender, leafy tendrils had been singed beyond renewal. To bring my poor plant back from death's door, I trimmed it way back, leaving me with a good handful of tattered but usable mint leaves, to which Ken said with childlike glee, "Let's make mojitos!" This seemed like a great idea at the time—not only did I hate the thought of wasting the mint, but I was thirsty and it was after 4 p.m. on a summer Saturday. Mojitos it was.

For once we had soda in the house (we can be counted on to have tonic, but not so with soda; I can't explain why), so I went digging in the liquor cupboard for the white rum. We don't drink rum as a rule, but I thought we had a boutique bottle of something hanging around. At least that's what I remembered. After thoroughly searching the depths of the dusty bottles, all I could find was amber rum, an unopened bottle of Santa Teresa 1796, something I'd obviously dragged home from work one day and unceremoniously shoved to the back to idle with the cachaça (carried back from Brazil over a decade ago) and the Costco-size jug of tequila (probably the same era). Not sure how big of a mojito misstep it was, I decided to try it; I mean, rum is rum, right?

Finding myself without a muddler (no real surprise), I had to improvise this part too and mashed up the mint using the wrong end of a wooden spoon. Feeling a bit like we had just built the Frankenstein of the mojito world, we took our first sips with hesitation. Our pause didn't last long. The amber rum added a toasty smokiness that softened the minty flavor and smoothed out the lime; while the color was unsettling at first—less refreshing in appearance than the traditional version—it was nothing we couldn't get beyond. Franken-Mojito was a keeper.

⅓ cup simple syrup

About 15 fresh
mint leaves

1 cup amber rum
(like Santa Teresa 1796
or Smith & Cross)

⅓ cup fresh lime juice
plus 1 whole lime,
sliced, for garnish

2–3 cups club soda

Lime slices, for garnish

Put the simple syrup and mint leaves in a shaker and muddle the leaves well to release the mint oil. Add the rum and lime juice and shake to combine. Pour the mixture into 4 ice-filled Collins glasses and top with the soda. Garnish with lime slices.

acknowledgments

A tribe of very special, thoughtful, and supportive people helped make *Graze* happen, all of massive importance to me and listed in no particular order.

Thank you . . .

Erica Clark, for making this book better at every single stage. My debt (and affection) grows.

Kate Schmidt, for being up for and excited about every adventure so far, especially this one.

Kate Jordan, for saying yes to an out-of-the-blue request, having a beautiful vision, and being the loveliest.

Nicole Franzen, for bringing your light—literally and figuratively—to this book and to me.

Dervla Kelly, for being the most collaborative, supportive, and inspiring editor imaginable.

Rae Ann Spitzenberger, for your stunning design, calming spirit, and irrepressible love of potato chips.

Andi Delott, for everything since circa 1983.

Jackie McCann, for all these years of unwavering belief, uncensored advice, and eternal optimism.

Frank Ottomanelli, for your contagious smile and for always letting me linger.

Jen and Jeff Meyer, Katy Anderson, Daniel Meyer, and *Gina Papalia*, for being the kind of friends who read a cookbook with the enthusiasm of a novel and then offer to do it again.

Evan Sung, Maeve Sheridan, Elana Hershman, Surfin Percy, and *Andie McMahon*, for listening, always.

Bev and George Rath, for being such good sports at the table.

Tricia Belvins, for your energy in testing and tasting. I'm so glad I found you.

Aly Mostel, Anna Cooperberg, Andrea Modica, Angie Giammarino, Amy King, Jennifer Levesque, Gail Gonzales, and everyone at Rodale for taking me on—again.

Angela Miller, for seeing the idea behind a word and helping to make it real.

Mark Bittman, for answering the phone, entering my life, and changing the course of it for the best.

My family, *Norm, Carolyn, and Ali Lenzer* and *Jeremy Yun*, for letting me highjack your histories so I could tell some silly stories about food.

And *Ken*, for letting me walk through this world by your side.

index

Boldface page numbers indicate photographs or illustrations.

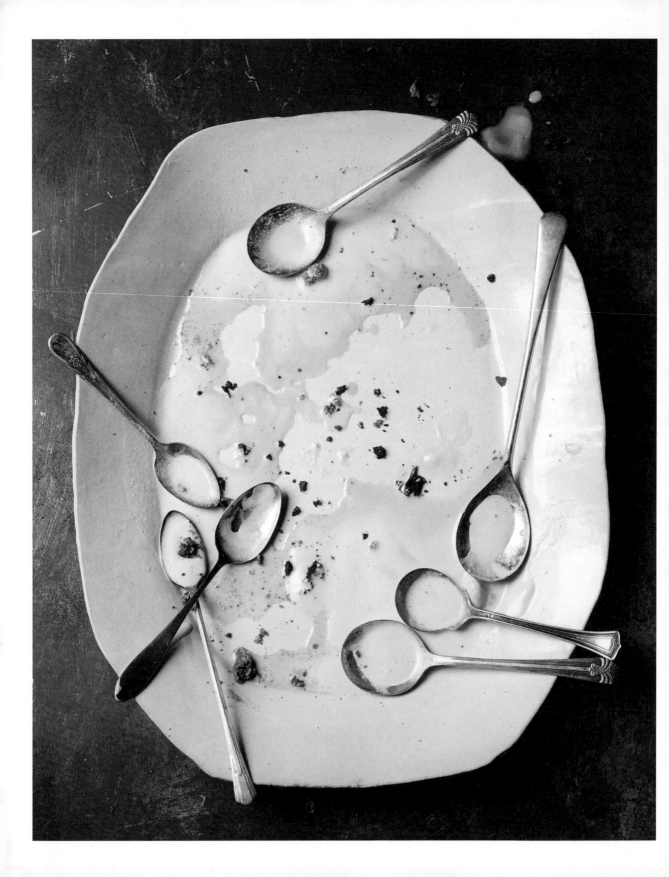